NO LONGER PROPERTY OF
SEATTLE PUBLIC LIBRARY

D0980690

MAN VS. BABY

THE CHAOS AND COMEDY OF REAL-LIFE PARENTING

MATT COYNE

SCRIBNER

New York   London   Toronto   Sydney   New Delhi

Scribner
An Imprint of Simon & Schuster, Inc.
1230 Avenue of the Americas
New York, NY 10020

Certain names have been changed.

Copyright © 2017 by Matt Coyne

All rights reserved, including the right to reproduce this book or portions thereof in any form whatsoever. For information, address Scribner Subsidiary Rights Department, 1230 Avenue of the Americas, New York, NY 10020.

First Scribner trade paperback edition April 2018

Originally published in Great Britain in 2017 as *Dummy* by Wildfire, an imprint of Headline Publishing Group

SCRIBNER and design are registered trademarks of The Gale Group, Inc., used under license by Simon & Schuster, Inc., the publisher of this work.

For information about special discounts for bulk purchases, please contact Simon & Schuster Special Sales at 1-866-506-1949 or business@simonandschuster.com.

The Simon & Schuster Speakers Bureau can bring authors to your live event. For more information or to book an event, contact the Simon & Schuster Speakers Bureau at 1-866-248-3049 or visit our website at www.simonspeakers.com.

All images courtesy of Matt Coyne
Interior design by Jill Putorti

Manufactured in the United States of America

10 9 8 7 6 5 4 3 2 1

Library of Congress Cataloging-in-Publication Data

Names: Coyne, Matt, author.
Title: Man vs. baby : the chaos and comedy of real-life parenting / by Matt Coyne.
Other titles: Dummy
Description: New York : Scribner, [2018]
Identifiers: LCCN 2017061761 | ISBN 9781501187414 (tp)
Subjects: LCSH: Fatherhood. | Fatherhood—Humor. | Parenting. |
    Parenting—Humor.
Classification: LCC HQ756 .C69 2018 | DDC 306.874/2—dc23 LC record
    available at https://lccn.loc.gov/2017061761

ISBN 978-1-5011-8741-4
ISBN 978-1-5011-8743-8 (ebook)

For Steve

Just kidding . . .
For Charlie and his mom

DISCLAIMER

This book was written by me, an English fella. We are two nations divided by a common language, so I've Americanized some of the words and references in the hope that they will make sense to an American audience. Should you wish to read the text authentically, please feel free to change *asshole* back to *arsehole* and imagine that the whole thing is being read aloud by someone who is pale and has dodgy teeth.

Cheers,
Matt

CONTENTS

PREFACE

When we first discovered that we were "expecting," someone bought us a fridge magnet. It read: "To have a baby is to invite an angel into your home."

That may be true.

But sometimes, just sometimes, it's like you have invited a lodger into your home. A furious, sleep-murdering, unstable and incontinent, breasts-obsessed midget lodger. Who wants nothing more or less than your undivided attention, from now until the day you fucking die.

. . . But that probably wouldn't fit on a fridge magnet.

INTRODUCTION

So, three months after the birth of our son, Charlie, I wrote a post on Facebook.

This is it.

Matt Coyne, December 7, 2015, 7:38 p.m.

I was congratulating myself today on how I've got diaper-changing down to a precision art. I'm basically like a Formula One pit crew . . . in fact, in many ways, I'm better, because when you're speed-changing the tires on Lewis Hamilton's car, he's probably less likely to piss in your eyes and projectile-shit up your arms.

This is what else I've learned so far.

The birth

- I used to think that the theory that the moon landing was a hoax was total bollocks, just because it required a huge amount of people to share a secret. I now think it's a distinct possibility, given the conspiracy of silence about how horrendous labor is. The labor suite is like being in 'Nam. It is nothing like you see in sitcoms or films, unless that film is *Saw IV*, or it's the chest-bursting scene from *Alien*. So, to those who told me that the birth would be a magical experience . . . you're a bunch of fucking liars. Labor is like magic . . . but only in that it's best when you don't know how it's done.

  (In truth, the hardest thing about labor is seeing someone you love in such excruciating pain. But then Lyns did once make me sit through an episode of *Downton Abbey*, so . . . six of one, half a doz . . .)

The first week

- I never knew this, but babies breathe in a jazz-syncopated rhythm. There is no set pattern to it and they stop breathing roughly every forty seconds, just long enough for you to think they've died. Of all the dick moves babies can pull, pretending that they've died is by far the most dickish, and they do it all the time.

- A baby crying is a weird thing. During the daytime you can listen to it and think that it's endearing and cute. . . . At 3 a.m. it's like having the inside of your skull sandpapered by an angry Viking.

- Baby piss in the eye really is only funny the first time and every single shit really is comically timed. The worst thing is when they do a "lure-shit," then wait till you've got the diaper off mid-change to bring the real thunder. It's the same thing terrorists do when they time bombs to go off just as the emergency services arrive.

- Every item of clothing is held together with fucking snaps. There are three or four more snaps than necessary just to make you look like a moron in front of your child, who shows his disapproval by endlessly windmilling. Dressing a windmilling baby is like trying to put a rabbit in a fucking balloon. When you tell them to stay still, they ignore you or scratch their own face. They're mental.

  (I'm thinking of launching a range of baby clothing that is all Velcro, based on strippers' trousers. You should be able to hold a baby in one hand, the clothes it's wearing in the other, and just separate the two with a satisfying rip.)

- Babies at this age don't look like anyone. But everyone sits around drinking a fuckload of tea and saying he looks like you, or he looks like his granddad or whatever. . . . In truth, they all look like Ross Kemp. (Well, they look like one of the Mitchell brothers anyway—if you've got an ugly baby, it's Phil.)*

---

*Ross Kemp is an actor who first found fame on the British soap opera *EastEnders*. He is the better-looking half of a bald and angry pair of tough guys called the Mitchell Brothers—Grant and Phil. (Just imagine Moby and James Carville side by side and jacked up on steroids.)

The first month

- Throughout my adult life I've tried to read a book a week or so. I'm not naïve, I knew that I'd have less time, so I thought I'd promise myself that I'd try to read a book a month. It's now been a couple of months and the only thing I've read is a pamphlet on breast pumps. (And I've still not gotten to the end of that; I keep falling asleep during the paragraph on "nipple confusion.")

- It is possible to have so little sleep that your balls hurt.

- Does anyone remember the show *Touch the Truck* with Dale Winton (before he had his face retrofitted)? It was on Channel 5 and basically eight contestants put their hands on a truck and the last one to keep their hands on it and stay awake won the thing. Having a baby is like being on *Touch the Truck*. The only difference is that on *Touch the Truck* you were allowed to have a piss and something to eat every three hours . . . and you won a truck.

- Whether Lyns likes it or not, holding the baby above your head when it's naked, and singing "Circle of Life," is funny.

- It's only when you've just gotten a baby to sleep that you realize how loud your house is. I thought our home was pretty quiet and sedate but it turns out we have a bathroom tap that sounds like Godzilla fucking a tank.

- Trying to walk around a supermarket takes ages because old women reeeally like babies and lock onto a pram with the dead-eyed tenacity of a predator drone. Dodging them is like playing Frogger. They're wily: if there's more than one of them you're screwed; they'll split up and hunt in packs like raptors.

After 3 months . . . now

The most important thing I've learned so far is that Charlie is supremely lucky to have Lyns as his mum. She's tough, smart, funny, and in love . . .

and she will make sure I don't fuck up too much. Hopefully, her DNA will also batter my genetic predisposition toward big nostrils and man-tits.

He is without reservation the greatest thing that has ever happened to us both. (Better than completing the Panini World Cup sticker album, which I did in both '86 and '90.) He has already removed enough of my cynicism to include this paragraph, and I feel pretty sure that I'm going to be good at this. Because as shit, disorganized, and pathetically inept as I am, it is beyond important to me that Charlie comes to no harm. And that, as far as I can make out, is not a bad measure.

I wrote this in a sleep-deprived state one Tuesday evening, when our little boy, Charlie, decided to close his eyes for a couple of hours, for what seemed like the first time since he'd opened them three months before. My balls *were* aching; I *did* have sunken eyes reddened by baby piss. I sat, I typed, I felt a bit better. And, as he stirred, I hit the "post" button and sent what I'd written to get trampled underfoot in the social-media parade of shocked-looking cats, dick-pics, and photographs of what Auntie Pat had for her tea.

The following day I logged back on to find that the post had been shared a hundred times. Later that day it was a thousand, and by the end of the week it was tens of thousands. It was shared by bloggers, vloggers, and even movie stars like Ashton Kutcher. Bizarrely, I started to get requests for interviews from newspapers, TV, and radio. And everybody asked the same question: Why did this incoherent and rambling "status update" strike a chord with parents, parents-to-be, and the long-haired one from *Dude, Where's My Car?*

I didn't know.

So I sat and I thought. Then I started to read through the e-mails I'd received from parents who had taken the time to get in touch. The answer was there. It was clear. There was a reason why this particular message echoed, why so many could find their own experience, in between the aching balls and nipple confusion, and that reason was as conclusive as it was striking:

INTRODUCTION

Most new parents haven't got the faintest fucking clue what they're doing.

Sure, there are the superparents, the bland routiners, the perfect assholes raising their cookie-cutter children using color-coded charts and whatever the fuck the "pick-up, put-down" method is.

But that's not us.

We are the screwups; the play-it-by-ear, winging-it normals; the inept, the scared, the disorganized, the immature and clueless. We have vomit on our shoulders and yellow shit under our fingernails and . . . Christ, are we tired!! . . . But we are Legion.

And our kids will be the kids that other kids want to play with. They will become the adults that other adults want to have a beer with. They will be the smart ones, the creative ones, the ones who will change the world or just make it better in tiny slivers. Because, as useless and pathetic as we are, our children will be the best of us.

Because we give a fuck that they can be.

1
ARRIVALS

The baby is coming. Shit.

Leaving for the hospital and I've just caught sight of myself in the mirror. I've only seen this facial expression once before . . . it was on the face of Hans Gruber at the end of Die Hard, *falling, after being dumped off the Nakatomi building by Bruce Willis.*

ARRIVALS

It was obvious from the moment that we set foot in the labor ward that we had been lied to. Everything we had read, every class we had attended in preparation for the birth, was no more than a Photoshopped picture. We'd been led to believe that a woman in labor would be like a delicate flower having a mild asthma attack, gently perspiring with effort as her natural pains caused her breath to catch. When we arrived, a woman down the corridor was in the later stages of birth. And she didn't sound like a gentle flower at all. She sounded like Hulk Hogan tearing the earth in two.

I was unprepared. We all are.

LYING BASTARDS

TV and film
There are two types of parent-to-be. There are those who want to be informed, to be made fully aware of the brutal realities of labor. And then there are the rest of us, who spend nine months in denial, preferring to remain blissfully ignorant about the truth of what is to come. It's easy to tell which sort of expectant parent you are because these two groups neatly divide, along the same lines, into those who choose to watch the TV show *One Born Every Minute* and those who deliberately avoid watching the TV show *One Born Every Minute*.* I was in the latter group. I did try to watch one episode, but twenty

---

One Born Every Minute is a popular docu-series in the UK that briefly aired in the US. It chronicles the reality of life on a maternity ward. (It's not one to watch while eating your dinner.)

seconds was all I could manage. I was left with one image carved into my brain: it was of a woman who looked like she was boiling, bent double and straining so hard that her forehead resembled a Klingon's ball-sack. I flipped the channel and watched *Beachfront Bargain Hunt*.

Apart from the occasional reality TV show, the vast majority of screen depictions of childbirth are complete bullshit, and as a consequence we all wander into the labor ward with a hopelessly skewed view of what the whole thing will be like.

Take something as simple as the position in which women give birth: every film and sitcom I have ever seen has the woman lying on her back throughout labor, legs akimbo, as if she plans to fire the baby out of her primed vagina-cannon. But, apparently, it is much more comfortable to be in different positions.

So, labor suites aren't how they are depicted either: they don't just consist of a hospital bed and beeping machines. More often, they have beanbags and yoga balls, sometimes even a small pool and ropes hanging from the ceiling. They resemble less a hospital room and more an obstacle course, or one of those wacky warehouse play-areas attached to family pubs in the UK for the offspring of piss-heads.

Far from the simple clinical environments we're used to seeing, the modern delivery room has dimmed lighting, a CD player, colorful pictures, a shower, and a place to make tea. If you include the screaming next door and crappy Wi-Fi, it's pretty much the same as staying in a Travelodge. The only difference is that there's no minibar and the previous guest hasn't wiped his ass on the towels.

Even screen depictions of how a woman goes into labor are a continent adrift from reality: in film and TV, a woman's waters break with no warning. A torrent is unleashed with enough ferocity to wash away bystanders and nearby cars and bridges, and babies are often born during the race to the hospital. In truth, waters don't always break, and labor usually takes ages. You might be tempted to call for a police escort or to speed to the hospital like you're in *Cannonball Run*, but unless you can see a head or a foot, the chances are you will be parked in the hospital for at least a day before anything really starts to happen. (While a second or third child tends to come quite quickly, the first feels like it's going to take so long he's going to come out walking and keen to crack on with his SATs.)

Books

Of course, it's dopey to think that films are going to accurately depict childbirth. No one is going along to the local IMAX for a twelve-hour birthing epic, seven hours of which are a woman sucking on a gas pipe, interspersed with her and her partner discussing how much the contractions are making her piles worsen. So most of us turn to a more traditionally reliable source: books.

There are approximately thirty thousand books on the market that deal with pregnancy and childbirth, and, speaking personally, we bought them all. As Lyndsay's waters broke, I was beginning to wish that I'd read one of them.

What was surprising was that Lyns *had* read these books, and she was similarly unprepared. None of them made much reference to the trench warfare reality of childbirth. Yes, I was in denial; but when it comes to books, from the experts to the idiots, so is everyone else.

Take this example from *The Good Housekeeping Guide to Parenting*. It says that giving birth is like trying to pass a "large piece of fruit while constipated." And that a woman in the second stages of labor will be "irritable." Now, far be it from me to point out inconsistencies in a *Good Housekeeping* guide to anything, but I get irritated when I miss a bus; I can't imagine it would be the same emotion if I had to shit a melon.

This book also suggests that a woman should pull apart her mouth using her index fingers to get "a sense of how much it stings." Three days of childbirth doesn't "sting." Nettles sting. Bees sting. Three days of labor doesn't smart, or sting, or niggle. It fucking hurts, and any woman who endures it is a warrior. . . . Any woman who does it more than once is Genghis Khan.

So, there are short, practical guides, with advice on how to breathe in and out. And long-winded birth preparation manuals that run to seven-hundred-page bricks that could better be used to batter a person into a coma (as if reading a seven-hundred-page book about "birth preparation" couldn't render a person unconscious enough).

But the truth is that almost all of these books are worthless, even the thoughtful, well-researched, and smart ones. Because, aside from anything else, if you've got a baby on the way, what the fuck are you thinking? You don't have time to read books. Including this one.

Childbirth classes

So TV is terrifying, films are bullshit, and books are confusing and too time-consuming to read. For an increasing number of people, the place to have labor demystified is at childbirth classes: a kind of remedial school for prospective parents.

Remember that class at school? Where they sent the kids who struggled with clapping and not eating the craft glue? It's a lot like that: a class in which they use words like *poop* and *pee-pee*, and everything is demonstrated using dolls and clip-art flashcards written in Comic Sans. The overall sense is that you've stumbled into a therapy class for people recovering from a recent head injury.

Basically, childbirth classes treat you like an idiot. But that's okay, because when it comes to looking after a baby you *are* an idiot, and the classes are designed, with the greatest of intentions, to teach you how not to be a total fuckup as a new parent. In some ways the classes are really good; in preparation for birth they are next to useless.

For understandable reasons they downplay the pain and trauma of giving birth, which is fine, but they do it in a way that causes utter confusion. Part of the problem is that they tend to be taught by new-age earth-mother types (ours was called Barbara, stick-dry hair, floaty dress, a whiff of zealous recycling, and a tendency toward bullshit). Consequently, they discuss the "birthing experience" rather than labor, and describe it in weird mystical terms with an emphasis on "spirituality" and "connection," which makes it sound like you are about to give birth to the last of the fucking unicorns.

Skirting the issue of pain, suggestions for labor agony focus on meditation, scented candles, and soothing music. Suffice to say, you come to realize how useful these suggestions are when you arrive at the labor suite on the day of reckoning, feeling that you are about to compete in *The Hunger Games* armed only with a Seaside Escapes Yankee Candle and a Coldplay CD.

So, when me and Lyndsay found ourselves standing in the reception area of our local hospital in the early hours of one Friday morning in September, we felt ill-equipped. And as we waited to be taken to the labor suite, I was pathetically nervous, but Lyns was understandably scared. We held one another and tried to draw on what we had learned from the library of books and guides we had amassed at home, what we had discovered from TV and film and childbirth classes. And we had nothing. Nothing but our fear, each other . . . and the reverberating sound of Hulk Hogan reaching ten centimeters dilation.

So, in hindsight, what is it that I wish we'd known?

DRUGS ARE COOL

During preparations we spent a great deal of time hearing and reading about breathing exercises, lighting, meditation, and atmosphere. The question of cold hard drugs was raised almost as an afterthought, which is bizarre, given that 90 percent of women will ultimately find themselves midlabor and pretty keen to get wasted.

So, for the purposes of reality: there are four main types of pain control other than the "imagine the pain as a doorway" bullshit.

1. TENS machine: Being told about these things was the point at which I realized how painful labor was likely to be. I mean, how painful is something if electrocuting yourself is considered pain relief? That's what this thing does. The mother-to-be has pads attached to her and the machine administers electric shocks. I had a go on this. It's exactly the same technology as those Slendertone abs machines that lazy people buy and strap to their fifty-four-inch waists in expectation of a six-pack. From what I've seen, neither works.

2. Gas and air: This is a combination of oxygen and nitrous oxide. I had a go on this as well. It's quite a pleasant light-headed sensation. To begin with, this seems to work. The woman giving birth holds the hose to her mouth and draws gently on it, and it definitely has a soothing effect. By the time contractions are seconds apart, though, it is being treated like the last bong in Amsterdam. It's safe to say that the effect seems to wane as things progress.

3. Opiates: In the US, the opiates of choice tend to be fentanyl or Nubain. In the UK we prefer diamorphine. Which is basically heroin. Better known as *brown*, *gear*, *horse*, or *skag*. But the good stuff. I didn't have a go on this because I grew up during the JUST SAY NO campaign (also, I thought as a dad-to-be in the delivery room, grabbing a syringe full of hospital-grade opiates and injecting myself with it might have been frowned on).

So I'm not really sure what taking diamorphine (or any other opiate) feels like. According to the babycentre.co.uk website, it is an injection in the thigh that, once it takes effect, inhibits pain and makes a woman in labor feel more relaxed. The downside is that, apparently, it also makes you feel spaced out and often nauseated and confused.

I think it's a lot like being drunk, but without the stigma of a woman getting halfway through labor and cracking out a sixer of Keystone Light.

(By the way, if you are also of the JUST SAY NO generation: having this one-off injection isn't addictive. This concern did come up in our childbirth class. But don't worry, despite what we were told in the eighties by those endless billboards and commercials, one hit of this stuff won't lead to your ass falling off and a lifetime of shoplifting from Kmart. Probably.)

4. Epidural: This is the daddy of pain relief. It's basically a tube of Jägermeister to the spine, and the effect is a bit like imagining Kelly-anne Conway naked, in that you feel absolutely nothing below the waist. Apparently, it can be quite painful putting the tube in and taking it out. But not having an epidural because of this is like refusing to have a screwdriver pulled out of your skull because it might mess your hair up. By that point it's probably true to say that pain is relative.

Whether it be a crack pipe, crystal meth, or the music of Neil Diamond, whichever type of pain control a woman chooses, there is no doubt that the experts—the childbirth gurus—regard some as "good" and some as "bad." One of the problems with the books and the classes is that there is this huge emphasis on "natural" childbirth: an unchallenged understanding that everything was better when women gave birth in caves by firelight.

There is a problem with this—it's horseshit. The facts of the matter are that when humanity was entirely reliant on nature, the outcomes for women and babies were pretty dismal, and peddling this "nature" myth just makes mothers-to-be feel guilty about even considering drugs to minimize their own pain.

And it's not just the "natural-is-best" mafia who promote the disavowal of drugs. One of the top midwives in the UK says that "pain-relieving drugs diminish childbirth as a rite of passage and undermine the mother and child bond." His name is Dr. Denis Walsh. He's a dude.

I don't mean to question Dr. Walsh's stake in all this, but it is pretty easy for a man to question the value of drugs for women in labor. In our childbirth class we were told that the equivalent of giving birth for a man would be passing a walnut through his penis. And, if that is even close to being true, the global population would be about seven . . . and most men (including Doc Walsh) would request an epidural on arrival in the hospital parking lot.

BIRTH PLAN VS. REALITY

One thing all the experts agree on is that consideration of pain relief should form part of your "birth plan." It's a weird thing to consider. Planning your response to pain is a bit like planning how you would react if a clown shit in your car: there is just no way of knowing until you are in the moment. In any case, a birth plan is best thought of as something similar to a New Year's resolution or a drunken conversation. The chances of it amounting to anything in the heat of battle is approaching zero. It seems reasonable at the time you're writing it, but you may as well be writing a wish on a cloud. So put what you want in it. Request that a baby Minotaur lick your feet during the whole thing, it doesn't matter.

As we were shown to our delivery room, we were still treating our birth plan with reverence, as if it were the Magna Carta. *This piece of paper will sort everything out,* we thought, with the blind optimism of Neville Chamberlain on his return from Germany in 1938. By the time Lyns was on the gas and air, it was stuck to the bottom of a nurse's shoe.

The average birth plan looks a bit like this:

BEFORE   AFTER

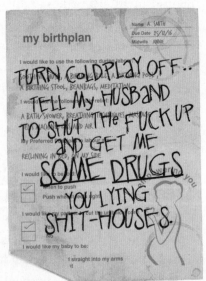

The above may be a bit of an exaggeration, but it is amazing how little of the birth plan survives the actual event. For example, your birth plan might start with selecting a midwife to take you through your birthing journey. But, in the UK at least, unless you are royalty or lucky, you usually get allocated one at random on the day. And probably more than one.

I always assumed that, from the moment urine hit a plastic stick, you would be assigned a midwife who would be your best friend for nine months. She'd be called Pamela. You'd get to know her kids, Michael and Tess (Michael's a history major at U Michigan and Tess wants to do something in drama). And she'd be a member of the family, always there, before and during the birth. After which, you would name the child Pamela, even if it's a boy, because Pamela had been great. . . . That's not how it works. We had three midwives and they apparated in and out like the Ghosts of Christmas Past, Present, and Future. So the Ghost of Christmas Past was efficient but calming (Claire). The Ghost of Christmas Present (Sarah) was really cheerful and enthusiastic. And the Ghost of Christmas Future (Annie) was miserable, and had a face that looked like a cat's asshole being burned at the stake. What midwife you get at this point seems such a big deal when you are completing your plan in the final few weeks of pregnancy. But it just doesn't matter. So long as the person responsible for mother and baby's health at that point is reasonably sober, and not Charlie Sheen crazy, nobody cares, least of all a woman in labor.

THE WAITING

The reason you usually have more than one midwife becomes ball-achingly obvious. Having a baby, especially the first, takes fucking ages. Time is relative, but the only thing that seems to take longer is the toaster at a hotel buffet breakfast. Childbirth is 90 percent waiting.

And waiting some more. . . .

But, strangely, this is unlike any waiting you have done before: it's exhausting because one of you is in pain, and both of you are bored and full of adrenaline at the same time. It's like watching a period drama on a plane that's plummeting to earth. For hours.

For men, most of the time you are in the labor suite your job is to be a one-man cheerleading team for your partner.

Within an hour most men have run out of useful things to say like "you're doing great," and they are already boring themselves and annoying the shit out of their other half. (There are only so many times you can say, "Breathe," without a woman in childbirth replying, "You breathe! You fucking idiot!!")

In fact, here's an idea to pass the time that utilizes this key feature of the birth: i.e., sweary fucking swearing.

PROFANITY BINGO

The rules: During labor the average woman curses seventeen times an hour, sometimes extremely creatively.

Simply check off the star in the middle if your partner invents a new swearword or uses one you've never heard before.

ARRIVALS

I was able to mark off the star with the word *fucktrumpet*.

Actually, Lyns was quite mild, with the occasional F, a W,* and a single quiet but menacing C. But on a trip to a vending machine I could quite clearly hear a woman chanting the word "C*nt" over and over, and another woman who shouted at her husband to "Fuck your fucking head," which doesn't make any sense, but was said with such demonic force I'm pretty sure the poor bastard gave it a go.

I never saw the woman in question, the woman in room "Acorn." But I did run into her husband in the parking lot, and he had the face of a man who had seen things that could never be unseen. As he returned to the room, I think I caught a glimpse inside of a woman upright in her bed. Her head was spinning 360 degrees, and the midwives were holding her down, while an old priest sprinkled her with water, shouting: "The power of Christ compels you."

According to our midwife, this poor woman had been in labor for four days, which is, to be fair, quite unusual. But, even on average, the first-time mother will spend eighteen hours in labor. I can't stress enough: labor takes ages. After thirteen hours, I started to feel a bit dopey for the way I had sped to the hospital, running at least one red light. (Christ, I could have pushed Lyns the twelve miles to the hospital in a shopping cart and still had time to stop for a Sausage and Egg McMuffin.) It seems ridiculous in hindsight, but most of us worry about this "mad dash" more than anything else. I spent most of the time in the weeks leading up to our due date imagining how I'd get a police escort should we hit any light traffic.

The thing is, we've all seen the videos and news stories of babies born en route to the hospital or caught one-handed as they free-fall out of their nine-month home, just as the parents arrive in the reception area of the hospital. But as Lyns entered the second day of labor, it felt as though Charlie was going to take so long to arrive he would come out desperate for his first pair of proper shoes. Like

---

*"Wanker"

13

so many first-timers, we started to wonder if this new-human thing was ever going to happen—and the midwife and doctor were starting to agree.

INDUCTION

It's around this time that everybody starts to talk about inducing. I'd heard of this before but wasn't really sure what it involved. I'm not a complete idiot: I knew that giving a baby inducement to arrive didn't involve hanging around the opening, waving about a bag of Haribo. But I didn't know that it was a chemical thing, whereby the doctor gives the mother a drug to speed up labor. (I'm not really sure what the new-age cops make of this use of drugs, nor what the natural equivalent of it would be. Maybe some sort of shamanic chanting and singing until the baby's head pokes out to tell everybody to keep it down and stop being such hippie dicks?)

Charlie was induced during the labor, but apparently it's exactly the same process when a baby is well overdue and shows no sign of turning up. In these instances, doctors decide it's time for junior/ junioress to make an appearance and the parents-to-be are called in and given an appointment. Like a baby eviction notice.

Anyway, it works. As soon as this stuff hits, the baby is packing up its placenta and is on its way.

A MAN'S BURDEN

It's fair to say that the next few hours are a blur, or at least my memories of them have been buried deep in a field at the back of my mind in a box marked NEVER OPEN. It astonishes me that some men say that being present during childbirth is the greatest experience of their lives. Have these weirdos never tried a Jet Ski? Miniature golf? Pictionary?

The simple truth is that a man's time in a labor ward will, more than likely, be spent watching someone he cares about in extreme discomfort. And, yes, the end result is life-affirming, incredible, and humbling, but this bit is crap. I would rather sit watching a construction worker take a shit than spend hours in this situation. Let alone sit there with popcorn, watching someone I love in pain, with a big grin on my face having "the greatest experience of my life."

After all the talk of drugs, breathing exercises, swearing, and candles, the main way that Lyns exorcised her own pain was by holding my hand. And when I say holding my hand, I mean trying to tear my arm off at the shoulder. The grip of a woman in labor exerts about three tons of pressure per square inch, which is the amount of torque that NASA uses to attach payload to the International Space Station. It's as though every bone in your hand is being milled to powder. But you can't feel it because all you can feel are the fingernails: holding hands with a woman in these later stages is only marginally preferable to holding hands with a jaguar while it's being castrated. But one simple piece of advice to any man reading this: this is an inappropriate time for you to mention to anybody in the room how much it hurts. Don't. The last man to do so died from toxic shock after having a Pilates ball inserted into his rectum.

As you enter the final stages of labor, most dads have been shuffling their chairs away from the area of action. If, as a man, your attempts at shuffling your chair have been really successful, you can find yourself seated on your own on a plastic chair in the parking lot reading *Popular Mechanics*. But for the majority of us, the most we can get away with is to find ourselves at the very head of the bed. I'm well aware of how pathetic this sounds to a woman who has experienced or is preparing for labor. It's not that we don't want to witness the birth itself, but we're squeamish and weak and at some point we've got confused between a stretched vagina and an eclipse, and think staring straight at either will make us blind. We've also been told by our non-father buddies that seeing a birth will put us off sex. (This is nonsense, by the way: by this time most men haven't had regular sex in so long that a lady area with shark's teeth wouldn't scare them off.)

It is incredible to think that according to the British parenting website babycentre.co.uk, 80 percent of men are scared of childbirth, a fear that exists despite the fact that the main pain they will endure during the process will be having to keep nipping out to put more money in the parking meter.

According to Mumsnet.com, the four biggest fears men have are:

1. Fainting

This is apparently a common fear, a sitcom classic, the response that can never be lived down. Actually, I did worry about it. I knew I'd never passed out in my life. I got dizzy once when I met Carol Decker, the lead singer of eighties chart-toppers T'Pau, but never fainted. So it's weird that this would get lodged in my head. But, if you are an expectant father with this fear, the chances of you passing out are minimal. This fear is just lost in the adrenaline and excitement. Unless you have the delicate constitution of a nineteenth-century gentlewoman who might get overcome by "the vapors," or you're one of those goats with a heart defect, the chances are you're not going to faint. Man up.

2. Being sick

Another common fear apparently. Again, it's extremely unlikely to happen. Neither of you will have eaten anything but chewy hospital toast for sixteen hours, so at worst you might dry-retch. Even if you can manage to vomit, you can't even begin to compete with the bodily fluids already flowing in that room. No one will even notice.

3. Cutting the cord and fucking it up

Okay, gentlemen, when the doctor offers you a pair of scissors and that weird alien rope thing, you're quite within your rights to say: "I tell you what, you went to medical school for seven years, you take this one, while I try to keep down the crisps I had thirteen hours ago."

Especially if you are such a moron that you think you might get it wrong. Don't take on the job if you're not up to it. Just imagine as you cut through that cord, the doctor shakes his head and says: "For fuck's sake, Dad, you had one job. . . ."

4. Sight of the placenta
Okay. Fair enough. It's pretty gross.
Anyway, according to the same survey, the number one fear a woman has about labor? "Health complications." And I think that this tells you all you need to know about why nature has entrusted childbirth to women.

THE FINAL PUSH

So, after what seems like a lifetime, everyone is exhausted. The mother is exhausted by pain and pushing, and the father is exhausted because it feels like he's spent the last umpteen hours trying to bathe Predator. (Again, men, for Christ's sake don't mention how tired you feel. No matter how tired you are, times it by ten and that's how tired your partner was yesterday. Mention any sort of discomfort on your part at this stage and she will use her last shred of energy to tear your penis off and make you wear it as a tie. The midwife will hold you down.)

And so comes the final push. A single burst of pure animal desperation. A primal, guttural scream of pain that has been heard a million times and hasn't changed since we were cave-dwelling Neanderthals giving birth by firelight, and caveman fathers tried to shuffle their rocks away from the action and into the cave parking lot.

I swear there was a moment of pure cut silence, before I heard Charlie's first cry.

And it felt like my heart and brain were taken out, rearranged, made better, and stuffed back in. I'm not a particularly spiritual person. I wouldn't use an Oprah Winfrey quote as a profile picture. But everything in that moment was heightened, everything was clearer. I *was* instantly less cynical, and in those moments I finally understood the sentiments I'd heard, an annoying number of times in the months before, about all this stuff being life-changing.

I'd seen the pictures of a newborn covered in the goop and mess of the womb, as though it's been swimming in a butcher's drains, and I should have been repulsed. I wasn't; I was mesmerized. And, as they placed Charlie on Lyns's chest, I knew that the two people in front of me were the most perfect of humans, and that I would love and protect them until my spine was dust.

We congratulated ourselves as the cord was cut on our old life, and I consoled myself with the fact that the hard bit was over.

. . . What a fucking idiot.

2

HOME

"There's no place like home . . ."

When you first become a parent, your home is just like Dorothy's house in The Wizard of Oz: it is suddenly picked up by a tornado and spun around in a dizzying mess. It's scary.

But after a few weeks the tornado abates, and the house lands. Don't ask me how, but it lands intact and in a world less gray. And your fear has not been destroyed, but it has been squashed just enough that you can barely see its stockinged feet.

But, fuck, are we not in Kansas anymore.

HOME

I could never understand why any woman would choose to have a home birth. When the idea was suggested to us and we were given the option, I remember thinking: *Mmm, decisions, decisions. . . .*

Did we want to have our baby in a building packed with health-care professionals—doctors, anesthetists, pharmacologists—and the most sophisticated monitoring technology available to humankind? Or did Lyns want to give birth on our living room floor, in a slowly deflating paddling pool, watching *Duck Dynasty*?

I understand the argument that home is where some women feel most comfortable, and maybe I'm missing the point. I feel most comfortable at my pal Don's house playing Xbox, but I wouldn't arrange for my prostate exam to take place on his settee. "Screw the hospital, Donald, this is where I feel most comfortable."

I thought the whole idea was insane. Still do.

But, as we prepared to leave the hospital, I realized there was one great advantage to having a home birth: when your little one is placed into your arms for the first time, you are already home.

You don't have to deal with the terror of leaving the hospital to return there.

And I was terrified of going home. Terrified of leaving the safety of the hospital and the supervision of people who knew what they were doing. It's a recurrent theme, but I just wasn't ready. I was under the impression that, having given birth, women stayed in the hospital for a while. (I was once again fooled by screen depictions of labor and stories from past generations about their weeks convalescing in hospital rooms afterward.) In reality, childbirth has become so routine that, as soon as junior exits the womb, winks, and gives the thumbs-up, there is no short-age of people handing you your coat and implying you should fuck off.

I tried to be reassured by this. Yes, we would have preferred a week in the hospital to process and adjust, to get used to the idea. But maternity wards are conveyor belts of raw humanity, and we were just one family among thousands about to fall off the end of the conveyor that day and into real life.

Handing Charlie over, and trusting that we knew which end was which, was an expression of the hospital's faith in us. It was time to suck it up. Ready or not.

. . . But as we walked to the car, with Charlie swinging in his car seat, I felt sick. I envisioned us at home and I saw myself as one of those monkeys at the start of *2001: A Space Odyssey*: a primitive idiot, scratching around in the dirt. Home would be my desert planet and Charlie would be this terrifying ever-present monolith . . . there to force me to evolve.

Going home was a leap into the unknown.

GOING HOME

Actually, as it turns out, it's more of a leap into a constant flow of tea and visitors.

Any fear that you will be left alone to get on with the bones of parenting disappears, as, for the first couple of weeks, your house turns into a drop-in center. A place of pilgrimage for a succession of relatives—some of them welcome, some of them not so welcome, and some of them you are surprised to discover are still alive.

Our living room was standing room only for two weeks. It was packed to the rafters with people, foil balloons, and strangely formal flowers, which gave the odd impression that someone had just had a birthday party but then promptly died.

Unlike the wise men and the shepherds traveling from afar to see the Messiah, these visitors may not have followed a star (they followed the GPS currently suctioned to the windshield of Uncle Brian's Toyota Corolla), but all are here to see and bear witness to the new arrival. And, absent frankincense, myrrh, and gold, they bring opinions, casseroles, and photos of their recent trip to Europe (it was nice, but they wouldn't go again).

It is said that a man's home is his castle, and this is a castle under siege.

A QUEST BEGINS

In those early days, as you try to adjust to your new home life, it's easy to think of these persistent visitors as a distraction or an annoyance. But maybe they serve an important role?

According to experts who study mythology, the story of "the quest" teaches us something so fundamental about ourselves that versions of it exist in cultures all over the world. The story always has a common theme: a journey in which the hero must overcome his own weaknesses in order to become a mature person, able to accept adult responsibilities.

So, maybe the visitors are aides in your quest to become a capable parent. Returning home from the hospital is your first step on this path, and, as annoying as these interlopers might be, it's just possible that each of them fulfills a vital role in the success of all erstwhile heroes as they venture forth.

So, here is a breakdown of your aides, the cast of characters now permanently occupying your living room. . . .

The Shaman

In mythological quests, there are certain recurring archetypal characters. Think of almost any book or film and you will come across them: The Hero, The Antihero, The Fool, The Shaman. The Shaman is a mentor, a teacher (like Yoda or Mr. Miyagi). A character who advises the hero and reveals the path. These mentoring characters are often depicted as oracles or wise old women. In your living room, these are the Nanas.

Nanas are the true tea drinkers. Capable of consuming vast quantities while seemingly never needing to urinate, they are characterized by their obsession with whom the baby looks like and their insistence on not giving you any advice . . . before giving you hours of advice.

The most notable thing about these handy hints and tips is that they are consistently in direct contradiction to everything you have ever read, or been told by a health professional. Advice from older generations usually consists of telling you that modern parenting is bullshit, germs are great, and in their day they had asbestos cribs and lead pacifiers, and they "turned out fine."

(Actually, they didn't turn out fine. Have you ever wondered why your parents and grandparents never know whether to click the left or right mouse button or work a basic remote control? It's not just because it's newfangled technology, it's because they spent their formative years licking formaldehyde-based paint off of their dolls' faces.)

Older generations are incredibly defensive of their ancient parenting techniques. But, while a lot of these old methods probably aren't as deadly as we are often led to believe, it's probably best to listen with a bit of healthy skepticism. Each generation has its own ideas and, generally speaking, those ideas have improved over time, otherwise we would all still be putting a couple of drops of opium in the little one's nighttime bottle. So, with all due respect to Nana, it's probably best to take what she says with a pinch of laudanum.

That said, there is something comforting about talking to someone who has successfully kept a human alive into adulthood without all the modern equipment we now consider vital when raising a kid. Think about it: she managed to bring up a baby without disposable diapers, baby monitors, microwaves, breast pumps, electronic thermometers, leggings, car seats, sterilizers . . . and the Internet, for fuck's sake!!

Let that sink in. She raised a child without Google.

. . .

Also, while Nanas' opinions on sleeping positions, feeding, and clothing would probably horrify the modern child-health expert, there is a welcome surety in what they have to say. Particularly as modern advice is so conflicting: Does anyone know whether swaddling is allowed or banned this week? Is co-sleeping lethal? Because it seems to be okay on US websites but not on their UK equivalents (which is weird—I can't see any reason why American babies are different, just because when they grow up they won't say the word *tomato* properly). The Nanas are right in one respect: modern advice is often bullshit, and trends frequently masquerade as wisdom.

And so, The Shamans are vital to our hero's journey. They have completed this quest before and traveled the road you are on when it was just a dirt track. Respect them, give them tea, and try not to argue. Even if their views are dangerously outdated, one day soon you will want them to babysit.

The Fool

THE FOOL

Again in quest mythology, there is the recurring character of The Fool. The comic relief. In your living room, this is the idiot perched uncomfortably on the arm of a chair, trying to look inconspicuous.

This was me before we had Charlie. The childless man. The most clueless dick in the room. In the presence of a newborn, I would become like an emo teenager, staring at my shoes and avoiding the fearful prospect of being invited to hold the new arrival.

Like a lot of men without kids, I just felt awkward and embarrassed holding a baby. I didn't dislike babies, but I was frightened of handling them all wrong and having a head or a leg come off in my hand. They just always seemed so fragile and susceptible to breakage. Also, I couldn't shake the feeling that babies had some sort of sixth sense (like a canary down a mine), and that if a baby burst into tears in your arms it was revealing to everyone that you were a bit of a prick.

Of course, everyone else in the room can smell this fear, which culminates in a seven-part comic ritual, which all Fools will recognize:

The Fool's Ritual . . .
1. Someone suggests/demands you hold the baby.
2. You try to avoid it.
3. Everyone then pressures you to hold the baby (with passive-aggressive comments like: "Go on, he/she won't bite," etc.).
4. You hold the baby awkwardly, as if it's a drunk squid, as everyone screams at you to "support the head!" like it was your fucking idea in the first place.
5. The baby cries . . . or shits . . . or vomits.
6. Everyone laughs.
7. You hand the baby back to its mum, feeling like a dick.

Of course, to avoid the ritual, the easiest thing to do would be to simply refuse to hold the baby when you are invited to. But, let's face it, no one is *invited* to hold a baby any more than you are *invited* to do karaoke. The more you refuse, the more the whole room thinks you're a miserable shithead.

I had been through The Fool's Ritual many times in the years before we had Charlie. And now that I've become confident about holding a baby without him coming to pieces like a Mr. Potato Head, I feel dopey that I was so averse to it.

In hindsight, I now realize there was a purpose to being The Fool, a help to the parents in their first stumbling steps upon their road. And that is to make them feel capable. Nothing makes someone feel better about their progress than seeing someone being more inept than they are. For a new mum and dad, seeing some clueless dickhead juggling their firstborn can be a real boost.

The Broken

THE BROKEN

The Broken are characters who foreshadow what is to come. A glimpse into the future.

These are the parents with multiple older kids, and they are visiting you and your new baby as part of a crippling schedule of kids' parties, karate lessons, and tuba practice.

These brave, weary souls are further on in their quest than you, and so the novelty of being a parent has begun to wear off. Consequently, they're looking at you like you've made the greatest mistake of your life.

They look fucked. Like refugees who have wandered into your home because theirs has just been bombed. They have lost that early adrenaline-fueled smile of the new parent and instead are wearing a vaguely haunted expression. An expression that doesn't change as kid one and kid two smash the place up, punch Uncle Brian in the nuts, and scream like they're trying to tear a hole in time.

The Broken are characterized by bits of banana, chips, and pudding in their uncombed hair, and their stain-hardened clothes, which haven't been washed or ironed since they had TIME: the commodity they crave even more than sleep.

They have the appearance of tramps, an impression not improved by the fact that they are looking for a suitable moment to ask if there is any wine. And, if not, does anybody mind if they open one of the bottles they've been clanking in a plastic bag since they walked in?

Every quest has a low point, and in your living room The Broken represent the darkest hours, a reminder that there will be moments in the future when it will be tough beyond measure. But take solace in the fact that, after everything they have been through, they are still alive and they are here to introduce you to one of your greatest allies in the quest ahead: cheap supermarket alcohol.

The Rebel

THE REBEL

Finally, there are The Rebels—the anti-heroes: the aunts, uncles, cousins, and friends who are too young to have kids. Or have decided not to have any children at all, simply because their lives are way too cool to fuck up on purpose.

Just as The Broken foreshadow what is to come, so The Rebels echo what is past. And as they call in to visit, on their way to or from some hip new bar or restaurant, they are a reminder of what is now gone: the freedom that comes with a lack of responsibility. They represent the carefree blowouts, the weekends away, the spontaneous parties, and that time you drank an entire box of wine and face-planted into a trash can outside KFC.

Rebels say things like "I'm not ready for kids" or "I love kids, but it's nice to hand them back at the end of the day." What they actually mean is: "It's nice to hand them back at the end of the day . . . because it's Friday and it's two for one on Jell-O shots at WildKatz. Good luck with the piss, shit, and tears. Peace out, you fucking losers!" And who can blame them? That was us, such a short time ago.

Or was it? It's years since we've been to a club (the last time I went to a club, the DJ was playing a floor-filler by *NSYNC). The last spontaneous party we had was for the 2010 season finale of *Dancing with the Stars* (I made lasagna). And, given the choice, I would rather watch *Storage Wars* with a nice cup of tea than go to an underground rave. . . . But that's not the point. We may not have exercised the freedom to live the lives of hedonist party animals before the baby arrived, but now that that freedom is gone, we miss it.

You will come to envy the carefree lifestyle of The Rebel more and more. But these free spirits are not visiting and taking up space on your sofa to make you feel bad about the life you have chosen. In these early days, their value to your quest is clear. Heroes take note: You must wave good-bye to your own rebel. Good-bye to your meaningless, shallow, cool-as-fuck old life. It is time to prepare for the new one. Your quest to become a functioning parent has begun, and every great journey begins at home.

HOME ALONE

And so, after a week or two, the living room encampment starts to dwindle. Eventually, the nanas, the cousins, the aunts, and the uncles sod off. And you are finally left alone to begin the process of coming to terms with what you've done.

This was the point at which I began to realize that my preconceived ideas about what it would be like to have a baby in the house were entirely inaccurate. And, in actual fact, were the imaginings of a naïve moron with a brain the size of a walnut.

What the experts had said about returning home was that there was an "adjustment" to be made as the first few weeks unfolded. This turned out to be a woefully inadequate word. Our new home life was an "adjustment" in the same way that the asteroid that hit the earth in 65 million BC was an adjustment for the dinosaurs.

If you're a parent, and you're reading this with a hot beverage in your hands, it's probably best that you put it to one side, as you're about to read a sentence that can only be described as "piss-funny." It was something that Lyns said as she contemplated being off work on maternity leave when the baby was born. She said, and I quote:

"It will be nice to have time to bake."

Yeah. That's how utterly blind we were to the realities of home life with a baby. And so, prior to the birth, when Lyns was planning to while away her time making brownies and cake pops, I was deciding which TV box sets to catch up on and what books I might read. We would both be off work for the first few weeks, so why wouldn't we take advantage of that paid leave? Why wouldn't we lead a brief life of domestic bliss while the baby slept a quiet, murmuring sleep, waking only occasionally to be contentedly fed?

Fast-forward two weeks, and we were shuffling around our home like gibbering shit-wrecks: Lyns trying to find the time to make a slice of toast, as I chose to forgo the reading of novels to read online advice about cracked nipples, and forgot about box sets to watch YouTube videos about the optimum color of milk shit. We didn't have time to make cake or watch *Breaking Bad*, any more than we had time to wipe away the stress-spit gathering at the corners of our foaming mouths.

By the time we'd left the hospital, we had read about the practicalities of going home and all the advice about what to expect. But what the advice had failed to convey is this: it's hard.

Really hard.

TIME AND SPACE

You cannot fail to be awed by the strength and stamina of a woman in labor, but her capacity for strength following birth is a thing to behold. Recovering from the physical and mental strain of childbirth requires sleep, care, and attention. But, in coming home, women find themselves in a place in which all attention (including their own) is undividedly on the new arrival, and sleep is just a grand idea. They carry the burden of feeding, the burden of comfort, and, in Lyndsay's case, the burden of my ignorance and stupidity. For new moms, the transition between giving birth and looking after a baby is seamless in time, but jarring in reality, like walking out of a car crash and being made to spin plates. For women who give birth, there is no recovery time because there is no time.

So it seems glib to say that it's tough for both parents. But it is. With a newborn in residence, your home instantly becomes a workplace. A workplace with the most intense pressure, brutal working hours and conditions, where you don't get breaks or vacations and no one wanders up to your desk, slaps you on the back, and says: "Hey, Bob! Great job today, take the rest of the week off."

When *we* returned home from the hospital, it was to exactly the same pile of bricks that we had left just a few days before, but we were now mommy and daddy, and consequently this was a strange place, a singularity where time was swallowed up in a daily gulp.

Time has no meaning here. You look at the clock and it's 7:30 a.m., then the next time you look it's Thursday. There is no day, there is no night. Just the distance between coffees and those blissful moments on the toilet when you get a breather.

For two weeks I didn't shower, didn't shave, and barely ate, and neither of us escaped from bathrobes and sweatpants. We looked like the forgotten patients in the basement of a Victorian asylum. And I smelled like a hobo had taken a shit in a shopping bag.

We certainly didn't have time to wash and iron our own clothes. Most of us have experienced what it is like to return home from a vacation and find that you have nothing clean to wear. For a few days you are forced to dig in the back of the closet among the dregs of your sartorial history. New parents face the same problem, taken to the extreme. During this period, I once answered the door to a woman collecting for Guide Dogs for the Blind. I had a thousand-yard stare and a beard you could bury a burrito in, and was wearing a *Star Wars* bathrobe, boxer shorts, rubber boots, and a T-shirt I got free with a

Kiss album, with the words *Pull the trigger on my love gun* printed on it. The woman took a step back as I opened the front door, looking as though she wasn't sure if she should ask for a donation or start fishing for her pepper spray.

She knew what I knew when I looked in the mirror: I was a man on the edge. And Lyns stood next to me staring into the same abyss.

Within the first few days of Charlie's arrival, we were wrecked. In the UK, when you leave the hospital with your baby, a health visitor regularly visits you at home for the first couple of months to check how you're coping. When the health visitor came for our first appointment, she asked us how we felt, and I replied for both of us: "Happy, but completely fucked." Lyndsay was so tired she didn't even apologize for my language. Our health visitor smiled politely and said we were doing fine and tried to reassure us that it would get easier and that having a baby was a "steep learning curve." Which is true, in the same way that Everest is a bit hilly.

First-Time Parents' Learning Curve:

The good news is that this period is as hard as it gets. After the first few weeks, it does get a bit easier. Coming home is a baptism by fire (and there is no doubt it burns), but you learn quickly and feverishly. And, as you develop your own system for dealing with the daily challenges, it becomes possible to carve out small fragments of time, to take stock and evaluate your progress. To put your arms around your partner and enjoy the tiny fingers and toes of your brand-new person and a life less ordinary.

The bad news is that your learning curve now starts to look like this:

And I'm not sure it ever stops looking like this. It's just a case of adjusting.

THE NEST

We thought we had prepared for this "adjustment." Or at least prepared our home. The experts call it "nesting," the compulsion to make sure that everything is perfect before the baby arrives. For most animals and birds, nesting means making the environment safe and comfortable. For humans, it involves turning that room where you normally dump all the crap into a nursery.

For most parents-to-be, the "baby's room" becomes a focus of this nesting impulse. Understandably so. Up until now the baby's home has been the womb, the most comfortable environment a human will ever experience. For your new arrival, the womb was warm and safe, and everything needed was provided on tap. The baby was then pulled, kicking and screaming, backward through a hole one-tenth the size of its own head, into a room in which everyone was crying and losing their shit.

The least we can do is make their new bedroom nice.

(The most obvious way to make the baby feel welcome would be to decorate the room as the insides of a person. In fact, I've thought about crowdfunding a range of interior wall coverings called the Living Womb line. Parents could decorate their nurseries in our "amniotic sac eggshell purple," with such features as "uterine lining" wallpaper. I suggested the idea to Lyns, but she didn't seem that convinced as she just mouthed the word "idiot" under her breath and carried on with what she was doing.)

Most parents decorate the baby's room in the most unthreatening ways they can imagine. With wall-stenciled alphabets and stars, fluffy toys, bright furniture, and welcoming gender-specific colors. We go to great lengths to make the nursery a cheery and colorful environment, excitedly adding more and more cutesy, adorable stuff. Until it looks like a suicide Care Bear has detonated its vest in the center of the room and its insides of clouds and stars and wishes and rainbows have been splattered all over the walls.

Whatever your taste, it has to be perfect; it's not until later that we discover that the baby probably won't sleep in this room until it is old enough to request that it be redecorated. And while this room is held like a shrine, the rest of the house begins to resemble an abject, cluttered hovel.

Babies just aren't compatible with modern living: it's all the stuff.

STUFF

Babies were fine in days gone by when trends in home furnishing tended toward filling your house with knickknacks, when a home was defined by its sideboards cluttered with photographs and ornaments. But modern living aspires to minimalism and simplicity. We read magazines and watch TV programs that talk about "clean lines" and "feng shui," but when a baby is brought into that environment, the closest you can get to feng shui is to put the diaper pail somewhere you can't smell it while you're eating.

Bizarrely, from my observations, it seems it doesn't matter how big your home is: the main issue will always be a lack of space. We live in a pretty average-size house. But, whether you live in a studio apartment or a mansion, whatever space you have will be filled.

Prince William and Kate's Kensington Palace home has fifty-seven rooms, but I bet when the Queen pops round for a visit, she's still tripping over a VTech walker on her way to the lav.

It's some sort of law of physics or mathematics that only applies to a house with a baby in it: $(As+Bs) \propto Vh$. Or, Acquired Shit plus Bought Shit is directly proportional to the Volume of your home. Nature abhors a vacuum, and never more so than in a house with a new baby in it.

To illustrate the impact of all this on a home in the weeks following birth, let's take a quick tour around the average three-bedroom home with a small baby in it.

In fact, my average three-bedroom home with a small baby in it.

. . . Watch your step.

OUR HOUSE

The Hallway

As we enter through the front door, you will notice the massive accumulation of stuff in this small passageway. One of the reasons we haven't been out much since Charlie was born is because we can't get past all this shit to reach the front door and the outside. This small thoroughfare is permanently full of the gear you need to be battle-ready to go out into the world: stroller, waterproof covers, changing bag, toys, car seat. When I used to come home from work, I would fling open the front door, casually toss aside my coat and keys, and stroll to the fridge for a beer. Now it's no small achievement if I can muster enough shoulder strength to force the front door open against the crap on the other side before clambering over it all in search of the living room.

The Living Room

Having fought through the hallway, we arrive, on our tour, in the living room. (Please ignore the people drinking tea: they are straggling visitors who refuse to fuck off. I'm looking at you, Aunt Pat.)

We spent the previous nine months emptying the local Buy Buy Baby store into this living space. And so bassinets, bouncers, baby walkers, and changing stations all jostle for space alongside the more traditional living room furniture of sofa and TV. We bought too much. I've cried three times this year: once when I first saw Charlie on a scan, once when he was born, and once when our Visa card statement arrived. We *definitely* bought too much. But then the relatives arrived with more. And as the first-week visitors trooped in with gifts and toys, and the offloading parents arrived with boxes of stuff they no longer needed, we squeezed it all in, and stacked it against the stuff we already had. Filling the space like we were playing Tetris.

The Kitchen

The kitchen isn't much better. Nobody has too much space in their kitchen cupboards. You fill the gaps over the years with novelty mugs and pint glasses you stumbled home from the local bar with. So when you suddenly require the room for sterilizers and stuff, you soon realize that your kitchen is tiny, and has all the storage space of a hobbit's ass. As you can see, every cupboard overflows and every work surface is covered with spoons, teethers, and bottles. And, because each bottle disassembles into sixty-seven working parts, you have to move thousands of pieces of plastic and rubber nipples from one surface to another, just to find the kettle.

You will notice the impressive Jenga stack of washing-up that reaches from sink to ceiling—no one's doing that anytime soon. Neither is anyone mopping the kitchen floor, the stickiness of which can be attributed to carrying a baby and food, tea, or coffee at the same time. The kitchen floor is a fine example of how we are discovering new depths of hygiene. It used to be that if the kitchen floor was shiny, then it was adequately clean. Now we accept it as clean if it isn't sticky enough to suck your shoes off as you walk to the dishwasher.

The Stairs

Careful as we head up the stairs. Even this area is not immune to the effects of nesting. Because, like a moron, the one thing I did find time to do before the birth was fit a stair-gate. You now have to open and close this bloody thing every time you walk through it, as if we're observing the fucking country code* in our own house. Obviously, this was fitted two years too early, and is just an additional obstacle in a house that now seems to have been designed by an idiot.

---

* The country code is a set of rules that you are expected to abide by when walking in the British countryside. The main one being to close gates behind you . . . so cows and sheep don't go wandering off.

MAN vs. BABY

The Bathroom

More clutter. Plastic baby bath, baby toiletries, and a menagerie of plastic floaty dolphins, ducks, and penguins. *SAFETY ANNOUNCE-MENT:* Please try not to touch anything in this room. On the surface it may appear to be fine, but, in my attempts not to disturb the baby, I have avoided turning the light on in this room when I go to the toilet at night. Consequently, I have been urinating in almost complete darkness in here since he was born. As I say, it appears clean, but I suspect that if you could get one of those forensic UV luminol lamps that show up urine, you could turn out the lights and this room would light up like a Jackson Pollock piss-party.

Bedroom One

As we take a look in bedroom one, please try to stay together. Bedroom one is now The Dump or The Overflow. The room where we put all the junk displaced when we created the nursery. It also houses anything else that won't fit in our other rooms, all the stuff we may need later, and also the gear we wishfully think we might list on eBay one day. This room is basically wall-to-wall shit. We used to have a drawer like this; now it's a room, floor to ceiling packed with Jesus only knows what. (When we first started putting stuff in this room, we did attempt some sort of order by packing everything into cardboard boxes. But, because this bedroom over-looks the driveway, this pile of boxes around the window just makes the room look unnervingly like the "crow's nest" from which Lee Harvey Oswald shot JFK.)

Bedroom Two

Bedroom two is our room. Mine and Lyndsay's. The two main purposes of this room have for many years been sleep and sex. Both of which have been suspended indefinitely. Not least because this is where the baby sleeps. It is recommended that your baby sleep in your room for the first six months, so that is the arrangement we have. An arrangement that makes the pristine nursery across the landing seem all the more absurd.

This is where we spend most of our time, so the room is best appreciated as a kind of Tracey Emin art installation of half-finished mugs of coffee, plates, discarded clothing, and general disarray. Half-open drawers spill their contents into an already chaotic scene, giving the impression that a yard sale has just been abandoned after coming under mortar attack. There used to be a children's TV show in the nineties called *Finders Keepers* in which kids were given helmets and fanny packs and invited to "raid the room," which basically meant finding prizes by ransacking the living fuck out of a fake house. Our bedroom looks like the closing credits of *Finders Keepers* if the kids had been allowed to prepare for the show by snorting bath salts.

The Nursery

And the final stop on our visit is the nursery.

An oasis of calm. A pristine monument to babyhood.

Which no one ever goes in.

(Ladies and gentlemen, that concludes our tour. Don't forget to tip your guides and leave through the gift shop, collecting your complimentary wet wipe to remove any stains you may have accrued on today's visit.)

So, apart from the nursery, in these early days every room in the house is a disaster zone. We lived in such order before. But now the whole place is crammed with crap and in such a state that it always looks as though we've just been burgled by bastards. For the first time in all the years we have lived in this house, there is a sense that the walls are closing in. And what was once a light and perfect home is now just a couple of trips to Babies"R"Us away from being as functional as one of those hoarders' homes where the occupants are found dead. Buried under an avalanche of unnecessary and useless shit.

THE PROPS OF PARENTING

And this was how our home was destroyed. Or became a "family home." And, sure enough, the house, congested as it was with cribs and toys and clothes and all the trappings of a young family, did suddenly look like a place where a young family lived. But, in a strange way, this made it all the more difficult to think of myself as a parent. It felt uncomfortably like we were surrounded by props and were in an amateur dramatic production of a family rather than a real one.

As I looked around at all our baby paraphernalia, I felt like we had amassed all this stuff in our home, re-creating the conditions of being a parent, in the hope that we would begin to feel like one.

But something strange happens while you're *pretending* to be a parent: imperceptibly, you realize that you *are* becoming one. And it's not the accumulated stuff that now fills your house that makes that happen. (You can't make a parent out of books, furniture, and toys.) In some ways, it's not even love or affection that begins the transformation into mom or dad. In those early days it is something much more scary. It is a dawning realization that you are utterly responsible for this infant's survival. He won't live without you getting your shit together. You quite literally hold his life in your hands, and it's okay to be scared because good parents are born and made in the fear of fucking that up.

NO GOING HOME

Here's the truth:

There is no going home. The home you left behind just a few hours/days before? It's gone.

What *we* left behind, when we raced to the hospital, was a home in which we could casually decide to watch a film, open a bottle of wine, nip to the pub for a quick pint, have a conversation, a shower, a piss . . . think.

Our home was designed to be a place of solace, a place of escape. But now it turned out that the thing we had spent so long trying to escape had followed us home and we had invited it in. And everyone knows that with soul-sucking monsters, the worst thing you can do is invite them in.

It just makes them all the more powerful.

But here's the thing: it turns out that monsters, for all their soul-sucking, can be a beautiful transforming power, and inviting ours in was the single greatest thing we ever did. Yes, our environment was changed. We had a great life before Charlie's arrival, and I'm not going to say anything as sentimental as it took him to make our house a home. Our home was already a home. It took Charlie to make it a bomb site, a wreck, a place where time is chewed up and we are spat out, a place of anarchy, chaos, and madness.

And who could possibly have thought that all this was exactly what our home had been lacking?

3

SLEEP

I fear sleep may not be on the agenda tonight.

It is bedtime, but Charlie's just given me that look that says:

"Well, Father, I have very much enjoyed my bathtime, I am more than pleased with the book you've just read (as you know, Zog is a personal favorite). And I am, as ever, enjoying the $27.99 Rainforest Friends lullaby lamp you purchased from Amazon. The soothing tunes are most enjoyable, and the combination of classical and jazz I've always found a great pacifier.

"That said, I think it's only fair to let you know that, despite your admirable efforts, should you try to place me in my crib this evening, I fully intend to melt the fuck down as if I'm being water-boarded by Iraqi police.

"I will thrash, kick, arch my back with spine-defying gymnastics, and generally behave as though I am being lowered into an active volcano rather than my bed.

"I don't give a shit that I'm tired: by the time either of us gets to sleep tonight, the neighbors will think that you're slaughtering livestock. So strap in, dickhead, for tonight we find out what you're made of."

. . . I'll pop some coffee on.

SLEEP

I remember the exact moment I realized that sleep deprivation was beginning to have an impact on me. It was after about three months and I'd just been caught staring at a woman's breasts in Pret A Manger.

Actually, I wasn't staring at her breasts, I was staring at the croissant on the cafeteria table in front of her. I'd noticed the croissant. Then I thought about how hungry I was. I then wondered how you make croissants, and then I began to think about what a funny-sounding word that was . . . *croissant, croissant, croissss-* . . .

I'd entered into what sleep scientists call a hypnagogic state. It's perfectly common when suffering from sleep deprivation, a state of mind in which you stare off into space and enter a dreamlike haze of consciousness. At least, that's what I would have told the court, had the woman at Pret called the police to complain that a pasty-looking man had just spent fifteen minutes staring at her boobs, drooling and mouthing the word *croissant*.

I must have looked insane. And in a way I was. Sleep deprivation is used as a form of torture for a reason. It breaks the spirit by assaulting the mind. It leaves you physically and emotionally wrecked and incapable of sound judgment and, ironically, everything else you need to be the functioning guardian of a small infant. (It also turns you into a baked-goods-obsessed pervert.)

SLEEP DEPRIVATION

Strangely, sleep deprivation is not specifically banned by the Geneva Convention. It should be. But even those backward societies that still use torture techniques think twice about using it as a means of interrogation. Not because it isn't cruel and unusual enough, but because it turns the subject into a useless gibbering fuckwit from whom nothing useful can be obtained.

Amen.

Have you ever tried to hold a conversation with the parent of a newborn? It is like debating chess strategy with a potted plant. It is impossible to obtain anything approaching information. They are incoherent. Their mind wanders like a child's. They respond to questions inappropriately and answer yes or no to questions that don't have yes-or-no answers.

If the effects of sleep withdrawal on a captured prisoner are the same as on a new parent, then any interrogation would go something like this:

"Where are the stolen nuclear warheads?"

"What? Oh the . . . [yawn], erm . . ."

"What is your mission?"

"No . . . I don't, erm . . . er, what?"

"Are you part of the Janus program?"

". . . er, huh-huh . . . [snigger] you said 'anus.'"

"For fuck's sake, let this dickhead sleep. When he wakes up we'll try hooking his nuts up to a car battery."

SLEEP, PREBIRTH

For years I have listened to and participated in those nonconversations that we tend to have when someone has a baby. The standard ribbing about the lack of sleep: "Are you getting any sleep yet?" "Is she keeping you up?" etc. I didn't realize how unfunny all that shit was. I mean, I knew these sorts of comments were never funny. But, now that I'm on the receiving end of them, I would place them on the funny scale somewhere between ball surgery and the CBS series *Two Broke Girls*.

I now want to go back to each of those people I flippantly joked with and apologize. Like most nonparents, I assumed that parents who complained about lack of sleep were talking about something simple: that when a baby is in the house, they wake you up during the night and therefore your sleep is broken and ineffective. But, in truth, it's not the night-waking that kills you. It's the month-on-month, cumulative effect of lack of sleep.

And the really shocking thing? You're already screwed before the little blighter has made its brutal, nightmarish, kick-the-fucking-doors-in entrance. By the time the birth comes, you are *already* sleep-deprived.

Maybe you are one of the lucky ones, or you're a sociopath—the kind of nonworrier able to get a reasonable amount of sleep in the nine-month countdown to birth—but it's doubtful. For most parents-to-be, the stress and fear of what is coming kill sleep like amphetamines. For the three months before Charlie's birth, I was way too wired to sleep; every time I tried to close my eyes I felt jacked up, as if I'd been mainlining cocaine or drinking Lance Armstrong's piss.

Practically, for the pregnant mother, just before the birth is about as uncomfortable as pregnancy gets. As Lyns describes it, "You're the size of a bungalow, your feet are swollen like clown shoes, and your bladder is the baby's hugging pillow." The nonpregnant one has a far lesser burden, but he is still responsible for getting his bungalow in and out of bed to go to the bathroom, massaging away cramps, and lying to his partner and telling her everything's going to be fine, when he himself feels as out of depth as an astronaut in a submarine.

This is all before the contractions start.

Prebirth is a sleep-free zone.

Then (as I may have already mentioned) the birth itself takes ages. And you'd be surprised how little napping occurs in a room in which someone is ejecting a mewling bowling ball through a vagina.

So, yeah, by the time the baby arrives you are already wiped out, already suffering from an extreme form of jet lag. But this is a jet lag where you never actually get off the plane. And the baby's here now. So, that jet you're on? . . . It just crashed into the side of a mountain.

SLEEP, POSTBIRTH

The NHS advice on arrival is to nap when the baby naps:

Try to sleep when your child sleeps. It might be tempting to use this time to catch up with housework or other chores but sometimes getting rest is more important. Set an alarm if you're worried about sleeping too long.

So there you go: Ignore those "tempting" chores. And take care not to sleep too long.

...?

What. The. Fuck!?

What parallel universe exists in which this advice applies? To anyone? The National Health Service is the finest and most noble of all great British institutions. But this particular bit of wisdom must have been written by a high-school intern, or someone who had randomly wandered in from the emergency room after a bang on the head.

If you were to ask a new parent if one of their concerns was sleeping too long, they would rank that concern right up there with fear of being abducted by time-traveling fruit. Sleeping too long? Not a big worry.

That said, part of this advice is repeated everywhere. Sleep when the baby sleeps. And, in fairness, on the face of it, it makes sense.

After all, apparently a newborn baby sleeps on average sixteen hours a day. (When I first read that stat, I assumed it was a typo, but it's true). So, if the baby sleeps for sixteen hours a day, and you are encouraged to sleep at the same time, you nonparents might be forgiven for thinking: *What's the problem? You lazy bastard.*

Well, the problem is that babies sleep in fifteen-minute bursts. The rest of the time they're feeding, or crapping, or throwing up, or needing changing. So by the time you've sorted out the devastation they have created in the previous fifteen minutes, they're awake again. And the longest spell of sleep you've managed since the day before was at about 2 a.m. when you remembered to blink.

This is what expectant parents don't realize. It's what I didn't realize. And it's because there is nothing to prepare you. I read a parenting magazine recently that had a long, center-page article entitled "Enjoying Your Newborn" that shared expert tips for expectant parents. Stuff like this:

Take the time to enjoy this period, it is a time you'll never get back.

And:

The joy of your first few weeks with your newborn are special. Pure treasure.

Mm. Before we had Charlie, I would have said that these tips were touching and sweet. But now I realize that this sort of "expert advice" is a denial of reality and offers nothing in preparedness.

Now when I think of that magazine, I consider it negligent. The author of "Enjoying Your Newborn" should be ashamed. Writers of this dangerous nonsense are Romans, their readers are Christians, and parenthood is a pack of hungry lions.

It all seems harmless, but at best, it is the pointless philosophy you find on Internet memes with a sunset in the background. At worst, it contributes to the feelings of inadequacy and guilt that all new parents feel. A sense of failure, just because they are not able to wander around as new parents with big dumb grins on their faces all the time, enjoying every minute.

You can't enjoy every minute. It's too hard. And, besides, enjoyment isn't a measure of love. Sometimes it's enough to be awake.

When, a couple of months ago, the same parenting magazine asked me for a tip for expectant parents, I sent them this:

Man vs. Baby
Top Tip #1
EXPECTANT PARENTS
...why not prepare for your new arrival by emptying your bank
account, smearing vomit on your shoulders & yellow shit under
your fingernails, and avoiding sleep until you think you might die?

I'll be honest. I haven't heard back.

COMPETITIVE TIREDNESS

Inevitably, in the stress cauldron of parenthood, new parents bicker
and argue, and the subject of sleep becomes the most bitterly fought
of battlegrounds. Competitive tiredness is the sport of choice for the
exhausted couple. You argue about who has had the least sleep, about
who slept last and longest, and eye each other enviously if one suspects
the other of having closed their eyes.

I'm not a great arguer but, when it came to sleep, I argued my
case with what I thought was conviction, logic, and coherence. I could
demonstrate with pie charts and spreadsheets where I had managed
to have less sleep than Lyns. After all, I was doing my bit at night, I
was changing diapers and helping with feedings, and I was still working nine to five.

But Lyns was working at home, twelve till twelve, twenty-four
hours a day. She had also spent the last nine months pregnant, had
gone through labor, and was responsible for feeding, all day, every day.

Of course Lyns was more tired. Of course our competition for who
was more exhausted was a noncontest. In the Olympics of our sleep
deprivation, Lyns was Usain Bolt and I was some fat pole-vaulter
from Kazakhstan demanding a medal for turning up.

But argue I did. A new baby is a live hand grenade, and a good
man would throw himself on it to save the mother of his child . . . but
I'm not a good man, I'm a coward. Not only did I not throw myself on

it, I would sometimes kick it toward Lyns and take cover. In my piti-ful defense, I was exhausted; my mind was mush, and it was defend-ing itself with spurious logic. My advice to any men going through this stage who are thinking that they are more tired than their part-ner: you're not. I look back now and realize that my arguments were the ravings of a lunatic, expressed with the conviction of a madman shouting at pigeons. I *was* tired. But not as tired as Lyns. I was wrong. This now hangs in our bathroom.

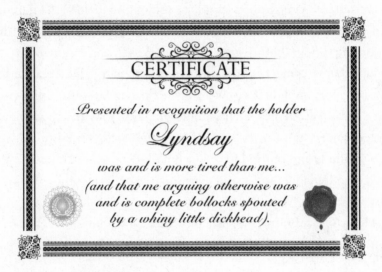

CERTIFICATE

Presented in recognition that the holder

Lyndsay

was and is more tired than me...
(and that me arguing otherwise was
and is complete bollocks spouted
by a whiny little dickhead).

. . . Lyns helped with the wording.

(Incidentally, not all couples have this battle. Just as I have met men who have never changed a diaper, I've also met men who have somehow avoided getting up in the night, or indeed avoided losing any sleep at all. I watched an interesting discussion "develop" between a couple at a wedding recently. The dad pointed to his twin girls: "No trouble with these two," he said with a glow of smugness. "They slept through pretty much from birth." To which his wife contributed: "Are you fucking kidding me!? They were a nightmare. *You* slept through from their birth. You lazy tosser." She then thrust the stroller at him and stormed off to the bar to get shit-faced. Leaving me and "lazy tosser" to shuffle our feet uncomfortably and talk about cars or something. So, as much as I was wrong to think I could compete in the arena of competitive tiredness, at least I'm not that guy.)

SURVIVAL

Just when we thought we couldn't be any more tired, Charlie developed jaundice. Which is apparently extremely common. (For those interested in the medical specifics, it's something to do with vitamins, and it makes you look like a character in *The Simpsons*.) Usually, this is nothing serious, but we were scared witless by the very remote possibility that it could be. So just when we thought that we couldn't survive with any less sleep, we did. For three days, we didn't close our eyes as we watched Charlie undergo blood tests and spend hours under sunbed lights in an incubator, as the doctors tried to increase his vitamin D and return him to the pink kid we started out with. We lived on adrenaline, stress, and fear, and our limits became new limits as we discovered what it is to worry, and worry hard.

He was fine. But, when pushed to these new limits, it was a revelation to discover how little sleep you actually need to remain upright and alive.

When people quote that often-used fact about Margaret Thatcher, that she only needed four hours of sleep a night, I used to think, *Wow, that's impressive.* I now think: *Thatcher was a wimp. Four uninterrupted hours of sleep? Iron Lady, my ass.*

New parents will survive on a fraction of that. Yes, they will wander around with the vacant expressions of people who have been taken over by an alien parasite that's drilled into their brains. But they function. They carry out the basic tasks required with the determination of exhausted explorers, concentrating on putting one foot in front of the other. It's not ideal. All new parents share stories about how they find their car keys in the freezer, or wander to the shops with one shoe on, forgetting why they went.

And, as I've already mentioned, having so little sleep encourages bad judgment, arguments, and general assiness. Thatcher might have survived on four hours for many years, but that may well have informed some of her decision-making. Historians trumpet her ability to need so little sleep, but historians should take another look. There's every chance that she stopped school milk, introduced the poll tax, and crushed the miners just because she was tired and a bit grumpy.

So sleep is important. And after the initial chaotic few weeks, there needs to be a plan. The key to ever catching up on the pre- and post-birth lack of sleep, to beating back the baby jet lag (and returning your fragile mind to a state of sanity), is first to get your baby to sleep through the night. Simple.

ROUTINE

POLICE INTERVIEW

Suspect: Matt Coyne. 12.11.15   Case No: 885089

Officer: Tell us, in your own words, what happened, Mr Coyne.

Coyne: Well, someone else stressed the importance of getting the baby into a routine, so I strangled them with my bare hands and set fire to the body.

Officer: Understood, you're free to go.

Get the baby into a routine. It is the number one piece of advice that you receive as a new parent. It comes from books, from relatives, from friends. It's a catchphrase really, and it is always said as though the person is imparting the wisdom of the ages. Oh, really? A routine, you say? I've never heard that before. We were just planning on feeding him and putting him to bed at random times based on fucking

rune stones or phrenology. We were going to let him have his breakfast at teatime, and his bedtime story at lunch, and wake him up to
go fucking kayaking at midnight. So thank you. Now that we know
to feed, bathe, and put him to bed at the same time every night, we
should be golden.

Don't get me wrong if you're reading this and you are one of the
43,619 people who gave me this advice: I did appreciate the sentiment.
I'm sure that it makes sense and everything, but there is one fundamental problem with the whole routine idea: the baby. Babies don't
care about routine any more than they give a shit about "quantitative
easing" or Brexit. Routine is for people who have existed for more
than six months. Routine is for those creatures who aren't frustrat-
ingly and fascinatingly different every single day. Sometimes Charlie
enjoys his bath, sometimes it's like we're bathing him in liquid nitro-
gen. Sometimes he enjoys his book, sometimes he wants to tear it into
shreds and force-feed it to himself. And sometimes he wants to sleep,
and sometimes he wants to keep you awake for days on end, until you
are hallucinating that your long-dead great-grandma Rose is taking a
shit in your downstairs bathroom.

SLEEP TRAINING

As I write this, Charlie is about eight months old, and I can honestly
say that no two days have been the same. We celebrate him sleeping
through the night as if we've achieved a milestone, only to discover
that he was just getting his energy together for the next four nights,
when he parties in his crib like we've plied him with PCP and cans
of Monster.

It was when Charlie was about four months old that this excruciating unpredictability reached crisis point and I did something
that up till then had been unthinkable. *I* deliberately sought out
expert advice.

The first thing I read was by one of the most eminent child psychologists in academic history, Dr. Benjamin Spock, who wrote:

By four months most babies are sleeping mainly at night, perhaps waking once or twice.

And I distinctly remember thinking: *Oh, fuck off, Spock,* and I looked elsewhere. . . .

The most obvious place to turn for fair, reasonable, and measured advice was, of course, ISIS.

ISIS

During our childbirth classes, there was a bulletin board in the classroom suggesting that if we had a problem with a baby sleeping, the best people to consult were ISIS. It seemed an interesting sideline for a fundamentalist jihadi death cult. But I looked a little closer and discovered that ISIS, in this case, actually stood for Infant Sleep Information Source. This is a real organization, stubbornly clinging to its name, despite the rather larger organization currently building a following in Iraq and Syria. "We were here first," I would imagine is the viewpoint of the Infant Sleep Information Source, and fair play to them and the head of their organization, Alan Qaeda. (I made that last bit up.) Anyway, despite the fact that Googling their name probably put me on some sort of MI5/CIA watch list, and that there is now a good chance I can't travel abroad without customs officers turning me inside out, ISIS did provide an interesting insight.

According to their website, when it comes to encouraging babies to sleep through the night there are two categories of techniques: preventative and therapeutic.

I think that's straightforward enough: *preventative* means "This is what to do so you don't fuck it up," and *therapeutic* means "This is what to do now that you've fucked it up." Naturally, we tended toward the therapeutic.

And these were some of the methods we tried.

Sleep journal

Keeping a sleep journal is quite a simple idea. Basically, you keep an hour-by-hour diary noting the times when your baby wakes during the night and for how long. This gives you insight into her personal sleep patterns. You can then time her naps and feedings better in the daytime and tailor her bedtime routine to her. One advocate of this system provided us with a diary to fill in, which included an example of the ideal twelve-hour sleep behavior of a four-month-old baby.

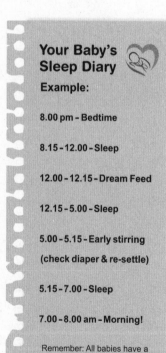

Your Baby's Sleep Diary

Example:

8.00 pm – Bedtime

8.15 – 12.00 – Sleep

12.00 – 12.15 – Dream Feed

12.15 – 5.00 – Sleep

5.00 – 5.15 – Early stirring

(check diaper & re-settle)

5.15 – 7.00 – Sleep

7.00 – 8.00 am – Morning!

Remember: All babies have a different sleep pattern. So don't expect to follow this example precisely. It is merely a guide.

Your Baby's Sleep Diary

Date: 07.25.

8PM: BEDTIME.

8PM –9PM: SCREAMED AS THOUGH WORLD ENDING

9PM–9.10PM: ARCHED BACK UNTIL HEAD TOUCHED ANKLES

9.10PM–9.14PM: SLEPT...FOR 4 MINUTES

9.14–9.25PM: SCREAMED, RAKED FACE WITH NAILS AND PUNCHED SELF IN TESTICLES REPEATEDLY

9.25PM–9.28PM: JAMMED LEGS IN CRIB BARS

9.28PM–9.35PM: SLEPT – 7 MINUTES

9.35PM –9.45PM: PRETENDED TO STOP BREATHING

9.45PM – STARTED BREATHING AGAIN.

9.45PM–10PM: SHOUTED WHAT SOUNDED LIKE THE WORD "MUUUUNG–BEEANS" REPEATEDLY FOR ¼ OF AN HOUR

10PM –10.15PM: BASHED HEAD ON SIDE OF CRIB

10.15PM–10.25PM: KICKED LEGS LIKE RIDING INVISIBLE BIKE

10.25PM–10.28PM: SLEPT FOR 3 FUCKING MINUTES

10.28PM –10.45PM: BLEW RASPBERRIES AND CHRIST!?... WHAT'S THAT FUCKING SMELL!!

10.4.6.2... LOST WILL TO LIVE

KILL ME. KILL ME. KILL ME

ALL WORK AND NO PLAY MAKES JACK A DULL BOY

ALL WORK AND NO PLAY MAKES JACK A DULL B...

We gave up after four days. Maybe we should have given it longer, but reading it back in the daytime, we found it was fast becoming the most depressing diary since Anne Frank's.

Baby hypnosis

I've always been suspicious of the effectiveness of hypnosis. Ever since Martin Bignall told me in high school that hypnosis was a great way to "bang chicks." Martin Bignall was fourteen years old and ninety-eight pounds, with heavy prescription glasses and acne that made God cry. If a "chick" had ever actually even spoken to Martin in real life, he would have imploded. Hypnosis didn't work for Martin, and as far as I can tell it doesn't work for anyone else. The only environment in which hypnosis seems to have any great success is on a cruise when the resident hypnotist drags a half-drunk attention seeker from the audience and gets him to eat a raw onion or pretend to be a chicken. As a technique for getting a baby to sleep, it's useless.

I did try it one night, though. Looking Charlie deep in the eyes, I explained to him that his eyelids were getting heavy in a calm, soothing voice. Charlie stared back at me and, to be honest, he seemed to do a better job of hypnotizing me than I did him. He stayed wide awake while I dozed off and woke up an hour later lying beside his crib, worried that he'd just had me clucking around the house for an hour trying to lay an imaginary egg.

The pick-up, put-down method

This method (advocated by the creepily named Baby Whisperer) stresses the importance of not rocking your baby to sleep. Instead you should pick him up when he cries and put him down again when he stops. Even if that's hundreds of times. The problem is you end up picking him up and putting him down so often you might as well be rocking him to sleep. You are simply rocking the baby up and down rather than from side to side. It's just semantics. The only value to this method is that it's a serious workout. Lifting and putting down a twenty-pound weight thirty times in an hour is a crappy way to get a baby to sleep, but a great way to build some ripped biceps. We tried this for a couple of weeks. When that period was up, we were more exhausted than before, and getting nowhere. And despite the fact that I'd developed some serious guns in the process, I'd also developed the posture of Gollum. As a lady with the username #PrincessAnne12 commented on the Mumsnet sleep-training forum: "It proper fucks up your back." (I'm not sure it was the real Princess Anne.)

Fading

Also called "withdrawal." The idea of the fading method is that you gradually wean your baby off the need to have you around so she can go to sleep. You do this by sitting in a chair beside the baby's crib, and then moving the chair a little bit farther away every night, until eventually you are out of the room. The theory is that the baby begins to go to sleep without needing you. One website suggested moving the chair back a foot every night. And here was the problem with this technique. I don't know how big the average nursery is, but ours is six feet wide, with Charlie's crib being two feet from the door. By the second night we were already sitting outside the room. Not so much "fading" as fucking off. Apparently fading should start showing results after just two weeks. Well, two weeks equates to fourteen feet. If we'd moved the chair at that rate, I'd have found myself, after two weeks, completely out of earshot and sitting on our neighbor's driveway, feeling like a bit of a dickhead. There was even some suggestion to persevere for months. At the same rate of fading, I would have spent the end of the first month passing the local post office, the second month the library, and within five months I'd have made it to the Baptist church on the other side of town.

The extinction method

For such a controversial method, you would have thought they would come up with a less aggressive-sounding name. It sounds like a euphemism a hit man might use. And, while taking out a hit on your baby would solve the sleeping issue, the extinction method is not quite that brutal. In fact, there is another, more up-to-date name for it, but it isn't much better: the "cry-it-out method." Like I said, not much better. The cry-it-out method sounds an awful lot like the "shut-up method" or the "suck-it-up method." (But at least they've got rid of the word *extinction* and all its associations with murder, death, and the genocide of endangered species for Chinese sex medicine.)

The cry-it-out method, or CIO, basically involves allowing babies to cry themselves to sleep.

We didn't try this. That is not a judgment on people who do. (It should be well established by now that I don't have the faintest clue what the fuck I'm talking about.) I know a lot of people who swear by the CIO method and their kids seem to be growing up without the homicidal triad of psychological issues: bed-wetting, cruelty to animals, and a love of setting fires.

From my understanding of it, it's not just a case of ignoring the baby's crying, it's about allowing her to realize that she's safe on her own. Allowing her to self-settle. (Which prompts the question: Why don't they call it the self-settle technique?)

I will say this: I don't remember how my parents dealt with my crying as a baby, but my mom always tells the same story. When I was a bit older than Charlie is now, I would scream the fillings from teeth to avoid sleeping. And one night, at the end of their tether, my mom and dad decided to let me cry it out. After an hour or so, all was silent. My parents were obviously delighted: it was tough to leave me to cry, but if it worked, it worked. As the story goes, after a couple of hours they came in to check that I was okay, to discover that I hadn't been sleeping at all, but had spent the previous two hours painting myself and the walls in my own shit.

I smiled and waved one brown hand at my mom, and I was never left to "self-settle" again.

*   *   *

There are a thousand other methods that sleep coaches and gurus recommend as they take advantage of your tiredness to pry open your wallet. But, in truth, they are all just variations on three basic techniques:

Technique 1: Don't let them cry at all—you goddamn snowflake.

Technique 2: Let them cry a bit—you pathetically confused, indecisive moron.

Technique 3: Let them cry—you inhuman, grotesque, heartless monster.

So, don't worry about which one you choose, you'll be wrong. Besides, judging by the number of parents on Facebook at 3 a.m., none of this crap actually works.

WHAT WORKS

As anyone who has researched sleep training in the wee hours of insanity will testify: sorting the shit from the chocolate is virtually impossible. No other subject is such a minefield of contradictions. When I first mentioned sleep training on my blog, I got messages with professional advice in droves. The first (and only) two I read began like this:

1. "Leaving a baby to cry is not torture. It does not cause stress or lasting emotional problems for babies."
2. "For a baby, being left to cry is torture."

When experts contradict each other so flagrantly, advice becomes meaningless.

I'm sure all these gurus who promote their theories have done a great deal of research into sleep patterns of babies. I'm sure they have carried out all kinds of experiments and have loads of letters after their names. You can tell. They start paragraphs with sentences like: "Young or old, as darkness falls your pineal gland releases the hormone melatonin. This sets . . ."

. . . Sorry, nodded off there for a second.

And this is one of the things that is so infuriating about expert advice. Contradiction really means: nobody truly *knows* anything. Not really. And banging on about the pineal or any other gland, when we're in a sleep-deprived state and want answers, is a bloody joke. Parents don't want to understand the science; we want a quick fix. We don't want to hear that there isn't a quick fix. We want one.

Expert: "Yeah, but there isn't a quick fi—"

Parent: "You're not listening."

So, there comes a point at which ignoring all the advice becomes eminently reasonable. When rocking a baby to sleep, or allowing her to feed when she wants, or even allowing him to sleep in your bed seems sensible. *I understand that I will be creating a monster, that in two years' time I will have a toddler who will never sleep . . . but so what?* goes the thinking. *If I don't start getting just a few hours a night, I'll be dead by then anyway.* And so we fall back on the things that we are repeatedly told are "the worst things you can do," and we do it purely because they work.

Pacing

. . . until your feet bleed. Picking a baby up when it is crying is often enough to stop it from being upset. Rocking it from side to side is the next stage. And if that doesn't work, the next level is pacing . . . until you have worn a groove in your carpet that resembles the approach to the dartboard in a dive bar. As an experiment, one week I put on one of those pedometer/step calculators to see how much I was pacing. I'd used one before we had Charlie, and on average I then did about thirty-two thousand steps every seven days. But, in comparison, here are stats from when Charlie was about four months old and refusing to nap:

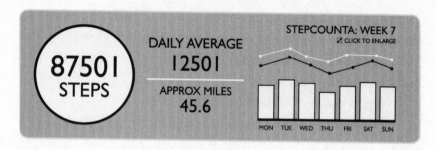

In one week, I clocked nearly fifty miles. I worked it out: it's the equivalent of me walking from my house to Grimsby (the UK town where happiness goes to die). Barefoot.

So it's safe to say that pacing is a bit of a drain on precious energy. But there are three big advantages to it:

1. It does get the baby to sleep (enough for you to be able to put him down, anyway).
2. It keeps you fit.
3. By pacing back and forth, rather than walking in a straight line, you never actually arrive in Grimsby.

The one disadvantage of pacing is that according to almost all experts, it is one of those "worst things you can do." "Pacing with a baby in arms conditions them to be overly dependent on . . ." blah blah. Shush, you'll wake him up.

The car

Realistically, there are only two reasonable explanations for driving around deserted streets in your underwear at three o'clock in the morning. Either you're frantically trying to dispose of the body of a dead prostitute or you are trying to get a stubborn baby to sleep.

Moving cars just work.

It was a few months into the battle for sleep when we discovered that putting Charlie in his car seat and taking him for a spin around the block had the same effect as chloroform. We noticed that when we were out during the day he would fight his daytime nap, but if we were going out in the car we needed only move a matter of feet and he would instantly be comatose, like a narcoleptic sheep. It occurred to us both at the same time: Would this work in the evening, as a last resort?

Sure enough, that night, when Charlie became unsettled, I put him in the back of the car and went for a drive. After less than five minutes he was fast asleep. In fact, so deeply asleep that when I got back, I was able to detach the car seat and carry it up to his room. And then simply pour our sleeping baby into his crib.

Convinced that we'd hit on something incredible, I went online the following day to see if this was a technique that others used; and sure enough, I found that millions of parents do exactly the same thing to get their kid to sleep. I also found it referred to in the expert advice as "the second worst thing you can do." For fuck's sake.

The reason we noticed that the car thing worked was because we had observed daytime behavior, Charlie's and ours, and it was quite a revelation. . . .

Daytime stimulation

When people say they "slept like a baby," they don't tend to mean that they slept intermittently and regularly woke up shrieking, soiling themselves, and tearing at their own face in a desperate bid to receive attention. When people use that phrase, they usually mean that they slept soundly and without conscience. Because babies aren't stirred by conscience . . . but they are stirred by everything else.

The lightest noise will stir a sleeping baby—it is the reason why parents ghost around the house at night. Why parents are transformed into nighttime ninjas—ninjas whose code of honor begins not with Bushido, but with an understanding never to flush the toilet after 8 p.m. Parents must learn to become one with their house, adept at avoiding creaky floorboards and that groany seventh step on the stairs, which, with a footfall, used to sound like a nun sighing, but now sounds like Björk being given a kick in the ass. To become masters of silence, parents must learn the art of withholding a cough until your throat is on fire and withholding a sneeze until you sneeze internally and it feels like you're going to shit your pants as your eyeballs explode outward. It is retreating from the side of a crib refusing to breathe and willing your heart to stop. Not long enough for you to keel over and die, but just long enough to stop making that infernal *ba-boom, ba-boom* that sounds deafening in the silence you have created.

Parents learn to communicate silently using eye movements and a made-up sign language similar to the one used by soldiers advancing quietly through jungle terrain. And just as the silence has been mastered, just as all noise has been tamed, just as the peace of stillness carries your baby into that restful nothingness . . . some bastard who lives next door walks past your house opening a bag of chips and it's all for fuck-all. Thanks a lot, Trevor, enjoy your sour cream and onion, you selfish prick.

In noticing that Charlie was happy to fall asleep in a noisy environment like the car, we started to think that maybe we were going about this whole thing wrong. Maybe we were being too quiet. Just maybe, creating an environment of silence was causing the exaggeration of noise that made Charlie wake up at night.

This is a blog post about that moment of realization:

The ongoing "Man vs. Baby" battle for sleep continues. . . .

Sshh, Charlie's asleep. But can anybody explain why when he naps during the daytime we could have a war in our house fought with brass instruments and he wouldn't stir . . . but put him to bed at night and a mouse could fart into a handkerchief forty miles away and he'll instantly bolt wide awake like "What the living fuck was that!?" . . . It's not that he doesn't sleep at all, he's just a lighter sleeper than O. J. Simpson's new missus.

The most infuriating thing is when he's fast asleep and I'm lowering him into his crib . . . or backing away from it . . . and my elbow or knee joint makes that bloody cracking noise . . . that's literally all it takes to wake him up.

To make matters worse, it turns out I have the body of an arthritic eighty-year-old. I never noticed before how much my joints creak and crack . . . ? In a quiet house, me attempting to move silently sounds like someone has thrown a load of damp wood on a fire.

So, we've tried "white noise," but trying to sleep in a room with a loud untuned radio makes me want to claw my own face off. We even tried an app with the sound of falling rain, but I was up for a piss every ten minutes.

I'm thinking, to make him sleep at night, we may have to re-create the conditions of daytime, turn on all the lights, vacuum, switch the TV on, and play a loud recording of the neighbors doing the recycling and me on the phone going apeshit at "Martin" from Comcast. I bet he sleeps like a log.

So, that's what we did. We re-created the conditions of daytime. If Charlie wouldn't sleep, we tried turning on the vacuum cleaner, the radio or TV, the washing machine or the dryer. And, incredibly, it worked. Everyone finally got some sleep. At least, until the electricity bill arrived, when we huddled together and wept.

SLEEP WILL COME

The subject of sleep is an obsession for most young families. In one survey, it was estimated that new parents lose on average twenty-six hours of sleep a week in the first year of parenthood. So no wonder we're all fucked, climbing the walls, and dreaming wistfully about being dead.

As we've seen, when it comes to encouraging your baby to sleep "through the night," there are a million differing pieces of advice, and I'm sure each person who offers their opinion is right. Their theory works . . . for *their* baby. The more honest experts will point out that there isn't a theory that works for everyone. As our lovely Spanish health visitor, Sylvia, likes to say: "There's no silver bully."

It's true. There is no quick fix and sometimes no fix at all, other than time.

With this in mind, a friend of mine told me the most common-sense, comforting, and sensible thing I've ever heard on this subject and it's this:

They don't sleep . . . and then they do.

It's not profound. It's not a conclusion reached by years of research or by experimentation on rats or puppies. This wisdom didn't require letters after my friend's name or a decade of study. But, nevertheless, it is true.

I can't help thinking that, if you happen to be trying out a sleep-training technique at the same time your baby decides to start sleeping, you will swear, from now until the end of time, that that technique works. It is human nature to see patterns and order where none exists.

And, when it comes to babies' sleeping habits, patterns and order are maddeningly elusive.

As I write this, Charlie rarely wakes at night. At around ten months, he just started "sleeping through." He didn't sleep . . . and then he did.

But for those of you still wearing out the carpet, joining the murderers for a 2 a.m. drive, or reading this book in the middle of a long-stretched night, I offer you this as truth, reiterated as a lamp of home and hope in the distance:

They don't sleep . . . and then they do.*

*(But they still wake up really fucking early.)

4

WASTE

This child produces more shit than Nickelback.

Seriously, if I put a copy of everything that Nickelback has ever produced in a garbage bin, I reckon that wouldn't fill it. . . . Three days of diapers and I can't close the fucking lid on ours.

WASTE

When the father of the atomic bomb, Robert Oppenheimer, saw the inhuman devastation his creation was capable of, he is said to have quoted from a Hindu scripture, the *Bhagavad Gita*. He said: "I am become death, destroyer of worlds." . . . I was reminded of this the first time Charlie shit in the bath.

Nothing prepares you for it. One moment we were enjoying "splishy splashy"; the next there was a scene of devastation. The kind of ecological disaster that environmentalists drag dead and gasping seagulls out of. It was a quagmire, and in the middle of it sat our baby, a miniature swamp-thing, still splishing and splashing and looking vaguely pleased with himself.

This is as bad as it gets. But 50 percent of caring for a baby is shit. Literally.

MECONIUM!

According to the NHS website, from the very first diaper change you should "try not to show any disgust at what is in their diaper, you don't want your baby to learn that doing a poo is something unpleasant or negative." First of all, I don't care what the experts say: a newborn baby hasn't got the faintest idea what "disgust" looks like. Secondly, on the whole, shit is unpleasant. Treating it like a friendly brown pet is going to lead to trouble.

With all due respect to NHS psychologists, I would be more concerned by the long-term psychological impact on a child of their parents grinning inanely at excrement, unwrapping a diaper as if it were a wedding present: down that road serial killers are made. So, despite what the professionals say, I don't think we should feel too bad if we open a diaper and look a little horrified. It's usually with damn good reason.

When first born, and for the next week or so, a baby craps out a thing called "meconium." It sounds like a made-up planet, or one of the X-Men. When I first heard the word, my initial thought was that I wished I'd known it when I was trying to come up with a name for a synth-indie band in about 1998. In fact (and this is about as informative as this book gets), meconium is the remnants of what the baby has ingested while in the womb: amniotic fluid, bile, mucus, an old boot, a bicycle tire. . . .

It is black. It has the consistency of tar. It looks like demonic Marmite,* or the sort of thing the devil would use to resurface his driveway. In fact, the sight of it will have you searching your child's scalp for a triple-six birthmark. Enough to say that it is disturbing, and on first viewing it is yet more unwelcome evidence that your baby is at death's door.

The good news is that after a few days the meconium stage passes. The bad news is that you come to miss the simplicity of these shits, as the next few months will be dominated by conversations about the variation in the ones that follow. What color they are, what consistency, what frequency, what they smell like, and how much one in particular looked a bit like Jeff Goldblum.

WHAT IS THIS SHIT?

So, apart from the Lure-Shit (see introduction), here are the abominations to look out for:

The Standard: Self-explanatory—this is your everyday, run-of-the-mill shit. Easily dealt with by a seasoned changer.

---

*Marmite is a black spread made from yeast extract (yum); it has the consistency of molasses and tastes like feet. The British eat it on toast, nobody really knows why.

WASTE

The Wrapper: This is a seemingly harmless Standard, but thanks to an ill-fitting diaper or the little one's sleeping position, the contents have wrapped around the baby's body, giving the impression that your child has been deliberately basted. If it wasn't you who put the last diaper on: apportion blame. If it was you: blame a faulty diaper.

The Phantom, or the Wish-Shit: This also has all the characteristics of a Standard—the straining, the sound, even the smell. And yet when the diaper is removed, there is nothing there. Don't worry. Basically, a wormhole has opened up between the butt and the diaper and the waste has left our time and space. (I've no idea where in the universe the wormhole comes out and where all this ungodly shit and horror end up, but I've got very good reason to believe it's the baby-changing facilities in the Doncaster branch of T.J.Maxx.)

The Hermit: As with a Phantom, the diaper is empty, but you can see the beginning of something on its way. You wipe and confirm it's there, but it's shy. Come back later.

The Expressionist: A fart/crap combo. The combination of pressurized air and waste can create a postmodern masterpiece. (Don't stand and admire—this could easily be a Lure-Shit.)

The Soup: The diaper has formed a bowl, and it is full. Don't just fold this one over: it must be held like a chalice with reverence in both hands and carried to the trash, or somewhere it can be poured, preferably over the back fence or into Mount Doom.

The Death-Shit: What characterizes this monstrosity is the vein-popping effort and strain on your baby's face, as if it is trying to lift a car. This is the shit that killed Elvis. And the realization of that effort is a thing of awesome power. If other dumps seem like a military bombardment, this is "shock and awe," as in the space of a moment your baby loses half its body weight. Do not attempt to clean this up alone. Call your partner. Christ, call the UN.

The Jeff Goldblum: Chances are you will never see one of these. This only ever happened to us once, but it did look a bit like Jeff Goldblum.

Of course, you don't have to memorize all these different types of waste. Things can be simplified by grading them according to severity. In our house we use a variation of the Richter scale. Anything above a four is a two-person job; anything above a six is a Code Red. Sevens and eights are Beast Mode.

We've never had a nine.

In the darkest corners of the Internet you hear about a nine. By all accounts, a nine requires haz-mat suits and renders any changing mat a hot zone with the same half-life as the Fukushima cafeteria.

CRAP EXPERTS

Whichever type of shit you have to deal with, the experts seem to ignore the fact that variation exists. Best-selling books on babies are filled with paragraphs that begin: "If your baby has soiled . . . " without acknowledging that the term *soiled* covers everything from a light dusting to some of the horrors discussed above.

There is a similar problem when the books talk, with characteristic delicacy, about "pee-pee." As the father of a boy, I thought that the tip about placing a tissue over his bits, to avoid piss in the face, was pretty good. But, again, this doesn't allow for the fact that sometimes he pisses like he's been on a bachelor weekend, and no tissue is going to hold back that flow. On these occasions we need plastic macs like you get in the splash zone at Sea World. And, apart from the tissue idea, none of the books suggest what to do when your baby has urinated so much that it has collected as a puddle in the changing mat and he is just splashing around in it like a cheerful duck.

In promoting the myth that all filled diapers (and babies) are created equal, almost every book on the shelf fails to tackle the truth of toileting—a failure often characterized by a ludicrously simplistic diagram of a placid child calmly having its backside wiped and its diaper replaced. It is with some disappointment that I always turn the page to discover that there aren't further diagrams showing a parent dealing with "shit-neck," or with the frustration of having stuck the sticky tab of the old diaper to the sticky tab of the new one. (I do this all the time. My record for accidentally sticking soiled diapers together is four. The result was a decorative chain that looked like the product of a deranged incontinent's arts and crafts hour.)

JEDIS OF SHIT

In fairness, parenting classes are actually pretty good preparation for dealing with all this unpleasantness. Most parenting classes provide a useful introduction to diaper-changing, but I for one entered into it thinking that it was probably a waste of time. I mean, how hard could it be to put a disposable diaper on a baby? Stupidly, with the brightly decorated diapers and sticky tabs, I thought it would be just like wrapping a particularly nasty present.

As part of our "Introduction to Diapers," I was partnered with another man, and we were given a doll to practice on. (I'm not sure why we weren't paired with our partners—it was something to do with reinforcing the father's diaper-changing responsibilities.) To add to the realism, hidden inside the doll's diaper was some sort of chutney to represent the waste. It was trickier than expected. I didn't undo one of the tapes properly, and as I tried to pull the diaper off, it snapped open, flicking a bit of chutney into Jeremy's mouth. Caught up in the role-play, he momentarily forgot that it was chutney and started to dry-heave into a nearby trash can.

This was an unpromising start to my own diaper-changing career, and Jeremy's partner was looking at him like she had made the greatest mistake of her life. (Which, of course, she had: over the period of the weeklong parenting classes, it became clear that Jeremy was a fucking moron.) But, despite a faltering start, over the next few classes we practiced, we got better, and after a while, we all felt pretty good that this was one skill we had mastered. We were the Jedis of shit.

Of course, the daily reality of diaper-changing made a mockery of this confidence. So as useful as parenting classes might prove to be, just remember: dolls stay still. Dolls don't piss in your eyes and crap up your sleeves while you're sorting out the shit they've just made. Dolls don't dip their hands in it like it's Nutella or grab the thing you're cleaning them with and stick it in their mouths. And dolls don't spend the entire time crying and screaming as if the world is ending . . . or, much, much worse, laughing in your face at how pathetically out of your depth you are.

THE CHANGER

One of the main problems is that there is no guaranteed way to know what particular travesty has occurred in a diaper without looking. By which time you are committed to being "the changer." Before we had Charlie, I always found it bizarre how a parent could be out for a meal or whatever, suspect a baby had crapped, and plant his or her nose in the baby's ass to check, breathing deep like it's sea air, and then casually sharing: "Yep, he's crapped." I now know that, with all the sophisticated technology that exists to measure every possible vital sign, this old-school method is the only way to ascertain if a baby has gone. But even this method is without guarantees. You can try to judge it by the smell, sound, or rumble, but in truth you could get the trousers off and find a Phantom or be staring straight at a nine.

There's also no timetable to diaper-changing: babies lack regularity. Like when I was a student and living on a diet of processed meats, they can go for days without any sign. Other times they're prolific. Our number one Google search for the first month was "how often should a baby poop." Amazingly, the experts said it was normal for it to be every five days, but also normal for it to be twelve times a day. How the fuck can both be normal? If a baby is a month old and takes a dump every five days, then he or she has only shit six times in his or her life; whereas if a baby goes twelve times a day, he or she will have crapped 360 times? I worked out that if you sat these two kids side by side in a fish tank and left them to it, the one on the right would have drowned them both before the one on the left had squeezed out so much as a teaspoon.

So, with this in mind, it's important to have a sensible approach to the division of labor. There is the simple turn-based "I Did It Last Time." Or the more controversial "He/She's On You" system. There are advantages and disadvantages to both methods. The I Did It Last Time method requires both parties to remember who changed the last diaper, and when you're changing up to twelve a day, this can be difficult. Also, this confusion can be exploited and the weakness of a person's sleep-deprived memory used against them. If your partner is on the ball and has the memory of a cyborg, then there is no escape from your turn. Lyns is like that, and in this scenario the I Did It Last Time approach lacks a little flexibility. A meteor could crash through our ceiling, severing both my arms and legs—Lyns would still look down at my quivering torso and say: "It's your turn, stumpy."

The He/She's On You method is much more flexible. Whoever the baby is on when he/she goes is responsible for cleanup. The problem with this is that it turns into a monumental game of pass the parcel, and your baby becomes a nuclear football. After using this method for a while, we found ourselves in a kind of escalating cold war of brinksmanship, holding on for as long as we could and then handing him off at the last minute. Incidentally, the key to a successful handoff is spotting "the face" early. In the seconds before an arrival, a baby's face turns a shade of red and his features pause in concentration as if he's trying to open a particularly stubborn jar. The trick is to hand him over before he gets the top off.

Whether you choose the I Did It Last Time or the He/She's On You method, there are one or two other complicating factors. Like what to do if the baby shits while independently in his crib, or on a stranger, or on a family member distant enough to tell you to fuck off at the suggestion that they roll up their sleeves. Anyway, considering all the information above, we ended up with a combination method that worked for us. I'm making it sound complicated, but I've condensed it into a simple diagram:

WHOSE TURN IS IT TO CHANGE THE DIAPER?

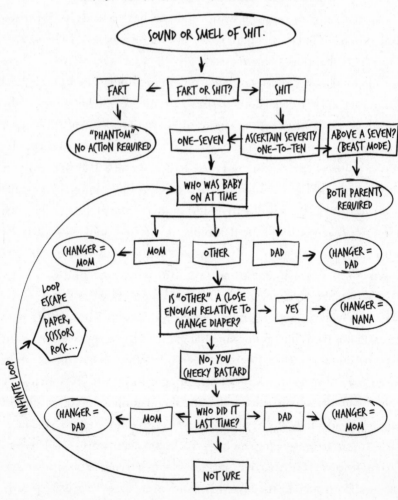

FROM THE REVEAL TO THE INDIANA

So you've assessed the damage and ruled out a Phantom, the diaper needs changing, and it is your turn.

When changing Charlie's diaper, I find it useful to imagine that I'm a player on the UK game show *The Cube*, in which the contestant is locked in a large glass box and made to complete challenges in a race against time, and host Phillip Schofield is standing nearby looking anxious but encouraging. After all, the process is in itself a series of challenges against the clock. From the moment you begin to change a diaper, the countdown has begun to complete the task before the next event. In fact, if *The Cube* were outfitted with pipes that sprayed the contestant in piss and shit as they lost a life, that would be a pretty accurate re-creation of the time-sensitive pressure enjoyed by the changer.

So, there are several parts/challenges to changing a diaper.

First of all there is the **Reveal**. The Reveal is characterized by hope. As the tapes of the diaper are undone and the contents exposed, a part of you hopes and prays for a Phantom—or that it is the merest shadow of a crap.

This is followed by **Denial**. Having exposed a travesty, you instantly close the diaper again, denying its existence and trying to return to a state of not knowing, like Schrödinger trying to shut the box on his dead cat.

Then comes the **Turnover**. This is a genuinely good piece of advice given to me by our health visitor: it basically involves turning the diaper over on itself to capture the mess in a kind of shit-calzone. This usually stops it from going all over your baby and yourself.

The Turnover is quickly followed by **Cleanup** (self-explanatory). And, having negotiated the Cleanup, we move on to a crucial stage of the change: the **Indiana**.

The Indiana is the most delicate part of the operation, as it involves the removal of the soiled diaper and the instant swap with a fresh one. It is exactly the same maneuver that Indiana Jones uses in *Raiders of the Lost Ark* when he has to switch a golden idol for an equivalently weighted bag of sand. Indy gets it wrong, and the shit hits the fan. Don't get this bit wrong or the shit will hit the fan, the walls, the carpet, and the dog. Seriously, if the thunder comes now, you're fucked.

There is one more step to take, perhaps the most vital of all the steps but one forever underestimated. The **Retape**. This is normally the time you notice that you've got the diaper on the wrong way round. It's fucking always the wrong way round. Always. It is almost impossible to tell the front of a diaper from the back. The back is just a bit bigger. Diaper manufacturers, in all their wisdom, have a tendency to put cartoon animals on both sides rather than what is needed, i.e., big letters saying the word "FRONT" on the front and "BACK" on the back. For some reason they think that parents are standing there, mid-change, admiring the frolicking elephants rather than thinking: *Please, God, be the right way around, this baby's going to shit on my hand.*

Of course, if you really are struggling with the whole diaper-changing thing, you could try the "no-diaper approach." Yes, this is exactly what it sounds like, and, yes, it is as insane as its name implies.

The idea is that, rather than making the child wear a diaper, you should try to spot when a baby is about to crap and hold him or her over a bowl or a toilet. This is an example of one of those bat-shit ideas that purport to be a return to a more natural form of child-rearing. Proponents of this method trot out the usual stuff about how we "didn't have diapers when we were living in caves." And, while that may be true, we didn't have fucking carpets either. The book *Baby-Led Parenting* says to expect a "lot of misses" as well as "the catches." . . . You don't say? The truth is, within a week your house is going to look and smell like a kennel. Instead of changing diapers, you will be mucking out once a week and wondering why all the visitors have dried up. (Incidentally, what the hell do you do when junior is roaming round Best Buy?)

This is just one of many bizarre theories when it comes to baby crap. At the beginning of this chapter, I mentioned how the NHS suggested that you try not to look disgusted when diaper-changing for fear that you will disturb your child. Other experts take this further, to suggest that you should discuss diaper-changing with your newborn, tell her that she has pooped or peed and why you are changing her. And that, if you follow these simple steps, diaper-changing can be a "lovely, intimate time together."

Well, each to their own, but I for one prefer the time when I'm reading *The Snail and the Whale* to Charlie, and I'm not about to feel guilty just because I can't treat his diaper-changing as a fun social event. Likewise, I'm not going to feel bad because I sometimes show disgust both by facial expression and by screaming, "Sweet Jesus of the fucking Orient, boy!" when I unveil a monster. I'm certainly not going to feel inadequate because I don't want to entertain the idea of our boy wandering around the house leaving shitty little gifts everywhere.

A BRIEF WORD ON TWINS

I'm well aware that some people reading this will be the parents or the expectant parents of twins. And they will chuckle with contempt at this whole chapter, and probably this whole book. Let me be clear: I am in awe of parents of twins, particularly when I think about the whole waste thing.

A friend of mine is father to two sets of twins, and when I spoke to him about the difficulties we were having with diaper-changing, he just laughed. He said that watching one while changing the other was difficult, but when they synchronized it was like *Apocalypse Now*. As piss fired from one, crap would fly out of the other. Changing diapers became just a containment exercise, like playing Whac-A-Mole. He made it sound like Armageddon. Another friend, Gavin, was there while we discussed this and came up with the simplest of solutions: just choose your favorite twin and let the other one sit in its own filth. Gavin doesn't have kids. But with that kind of problem-solving acumen, he's going to make a hell of a father one day.

SO . . .

It is never more obvious than when you're changing a diaper just how pathetic the human infant is. Other species are born running, able to take shelter and recognize danger, to communicate and understand. But a baby is utterly reliant on you. It is incapable of anything, other than eating, excreting, and blowing spit bubbles.

Realizing that you are genuinely responsible for the most basic needs of a small human is overwhelming, but dealing with the piss and shit of parenting is as much a measure of your love for them as how much you fling them around and sing about farm animals.

And, just remember, as your child lies there on its changing mat, flailing its arms around and dipping its socked feet in its own excrement, that one day you may yourself be in this infant state again: when age and infirmity throw their cloak over your wizened body, time completes its inexorable circle, and the child becomes father to the man.

And when that day comes for me, and Charlie finds himself now responsible for *my* most basic of needs, it will be with a glint in my ancient eye and revenge in my heart that I seize that opportunity . . .

And shit myself.

5

FEEDING

When it comes to feeding your baby . . . the world has an opinion.

You could read the vast amounts of academic research into childhood obesity, obsess over the hand-wringing advice of nutritionists, and find yourself surrounded by color-coded charts measuring the salt and sugar intake of every morsel of organic food that passes your baby's lips.

But it boils down to this:

Breast-feed if you can. Don't worry if you can't. And when the little one moves to solid foods, try not to feed them mashed-up Cheetos and a Twix all the time. Otherwise, they'll end up as fat and stupid as someone who thinks that feeding their kid Cheetos and a Twix all the time is okay.

FEEDING

There are moments in the first year of being a parent that strike you as odd. Moments that make you realize how much of early parenting is hidden from the public gaze. And moments that are just plain surreal.

For me, one such moment was walking into our bedroom one afternoon to find my partner of twenty years hooked up to the mains and being milked by a Willy Wonka–esque machine.

An electric breast pump is basically that: a milking machine, apparently designed by a fetishistic, mad genius.

In among all our other prebirth purchases, I did vaguely remember us buying this thing. But seeing it hooked up and in action was something else. All I could see were wires and tubes, which were in turn attached to a comically shaped funnel, which Lyns then held to her breast. With the accompanying rhythmic sucking, pumping sound, it looked a bit like she was playing an obscure Eastern European musical instrument.

(In fact, the noise it makes is quite pleasant. After I'd gotten accustomed to the strangeness, my next thought was that if I could teach Lyns to play the harmonica and pop a couple of cymbals between her legs, we might really be onto something.)

As it turns out, seeing a breast pump in action is one of the least weird things you can encounter in the bizarre world of baby-feeding. Which is saying something. What's really strange are the opinions, judgments, and oddball attitudes of the know-it-alls, the hurtful, the disturbed, and the just plain thick.

Now, *that's* weird.

BOTTLE OR BREAST

In March 2016, celebrity chef Jamie Oliver shared his opinion on the merits of breast-feeding. He suggested that choosing not to breast-feed can lead to general horror for your baby. Things like stunting, obesity, and ill health.

In fairness to him, Oliver was commenting on this stuff with the best of intentions. But he was blissfully unaware that he was stumbling into the ultimate parenting minefield: the subject of bottle or breast. And, as a backlash gathered momentum, he began to realize that it would have been marginally less controversial to release a cookbook with doodles of Muhammad in the margins.

He went on to say that breast-feeding reduces the risk of breast cancer and is convenient, nutritious, better than formula in every way, and free. Now, all of that may be true, but when he described it as "easy," he was immediately set upon—by a group of people who argued that their opinions were more valid than those of a guy who cooks on television: i.e., women. And, more specifically, women . . . who had actual breasts . . . and had actually tried to feed babies using them.

It isn't easy. From what I've seen, it can be incredibly hard and quite often impossible.

I think most people understand the "breast is best" theory. In fact, Lyns does breast-feed Charlie, but to say it is easy is just not true. And, from the experiences of others I've spoken to, breast may not necessarily be best if the soul-destroying effort of it drives you slowly insane, or contributes to that hatefully common Dementor of new moms: depression.

I'm not saying breast-feeding isn't a good thing, but there are a thousand factors that affect how healthily a child grows, and maybe the mental health of the mom is bigger than them all.

And anyway, *I* was bottle-fed. I'm still alive, I'm not obese, I don't steal women's shoes, I'm not three foot two, I survived. Incidentally, ask around among your friends. If you can tell the difference between those who were bottle-fed and those who were breast-fed, I'd be amazed. For all the well-intentioned commentary about the benefits of breast-feeding, it is safe to say that it's all a bit more complicated than that. Otherwise, when babies become adults, "breast is best" campaigners would be able to prove their point by putting a selection of people in a room and identifying them easily: the breast-fed ones by their glowing skin and six-packs, and the bottle-fed ones by their rickets and missing teeth.

EASY?

In my ignorance prior to being a dad, I also thought that breast-feeding was straightforward stuff. I thought that the process of feeding a baby was an example of elegance in the design of evolution. That nature had provided women with this natural, permanent source of food for their offspring: readily available, readily accessible, with nipply bits perfectly formed to the shape of a baby's lips. In my infinite dimness, I assumed that to all intents and purposes feeding infants involved popping a nipple in their mouth, right up until the day they started to demand chicken nuggets. But, in reality, the design is flawed. Babies don't seem to realize that their lips are "perfectly formed" or indeed that they need to feed at all. Babies are born utterly clueless of all these things and need to be taught. The problem is, they're only very recently alive so are not really in the mood to learn.

The drive to encourage women to breast-feed begins in the hospital, when a nipple becomes the focal point of everyone in the room—apart from the baby, who after all those years of evolution still just truffles around like a blind pig, lolling his head about until the pointy bit is near his mouth. He then looks like he's about to "latch on" (a delicate term that evokes images of hooking up a U-Haul to a tow bar), but at the last minute he veers away, lolling his head around again for a bit, as everybody oohs and aahs as if he's just missed an open goal.

The beautiful, simple dignity of a breast-feeding baby is for later, as during this orientation period he or she doesn't seem to have a clue, and displays all the dignity of a fish trying to hump a door.

Apparently, there are loads of reasons why babies struggle to start breast-feeding. Sometimes the milk doesn't come, or they struggle to latch on, or they don't have a strong sucking reflex, or fuck knows, they can't be bothered. We became familiar with all of the reasons during those early, frustrating days of trying to get Charlie to do what is supposed to come naturally. In the end we were just willing him to "get it." But it was a bit like trying to set up Wi-Fi when none of the bits of equipment will speak to each other. We knew the passwords were right, all the flashy lights were on . . . it just wouldn't work.

Finally, any shred of dignity that remained was removed by an old-hand nurse who started to manhandle Lyns's tits like a farmer encouraging a reluctant cow. Ruddy-faced and no-nonsense, Nurse Bennett seemed at one point like she was about to pull up a three-legged stool and start to try to fill a bucket, slapping Lyns on the rump with an "atta girl" at the slightest drop.

But he got it. Suddenly, Charlie got it. And it was a moment of triumph.

It seems strange to look back now and think that it was such a difficult process. Now Charlie breast-feeds like an old soak swanning up to the bar with a brandy glass. But for Lyns, as for most women, it was tough.

What I'm not looking forward to now is him stopping. Apparently, after all that effort, babies really don't want to give up on breast-feeding. And the advice about getting a baby off the breast isn't much better than "Plant one foot firmly on the floor, one foot on mum's chest, grab the kid by the ankles, and pull as hard as you can."

BREAST-FEEDING AND THE WEIRDOS

If there is a certain amount of controversy about choosing between bottle and breast and how "easy" it is to choose the latter, this is nothing by comparison to the controversy that surrounds breast-feeding in public. Every few months some celebrity will chime in about how they find it "disgusting." Or some backward restaurant or hotel will destroy its own TripAdvisor rating by demanding some poor woman "cover up" (as though she's naked and streaking past the buffet rather than feeding a baby).

In the UK, comments from Fox News commentator Katie Hopkins about breast-feeding women are typical:

They don't have the right to put everyone else off having milk in their tea. Put it away, girls.

The UK's biggest Trump fan, Nigel Farage, apparently agreed when he suggested that maybe breast-feeding women should "sit in a corner."

How about that moral arbiter of good taste, porn star and topless model Katie Price? Who despite being permanently exposed herself said:

I don't want to eat my dinner and see a woman's boob out.

Which is a bit rich given that, for the best part of a decade, the whole of the UK hasn't been able to have so much as a round of toast without seeing hers on TV or in a newspaper.

Even social philosopher Kim Kardashian has waded into the debate, using her notoriously wide-ranging vocabulary to tweet "Ew," when a woman began breast-feeding near her.

Ew, indeed.

There is something monumentally depressing about a woman making a great effort to feed her baby and then being discouraged by these odd opinions and very public declarations of disgust. And, to be honest, I genuinely thought that, in real life, this discouragement was a myth. That realistically, apart from a few rare examples, there was no way that people who held these views actually existed . . . and then you realize that they do.

I wrote about the moment I found this out on the *Man vs. Baby* blog:

Breast-feeding and the Weirdos

I know this has probably all been said before, but who are these fucking crackpots who have a problem with breast-feeding in public? Or these weirdos who say they "don't mind it" as long as it's done "discreetly."

Erm . . . show of hands . . . has anyone ever seen breast-feeding done indiscreetly? I for one have never seen a woman begin breast-feeding by ostentatiously unveiling her nipple-tasseled tits to the hard-house remix of "Here Comes the Boom." Or attach her baby to a rotating target and, to drumrolls, squirt-fire the milk at the child from six feet away.

In fact, come to think of it, I've never even seen a nipple when a woman has been breast-feeding because . . . (and here's the science bit) . . . that's what the baby feeds from. So, the nipple is, by its very design, covered by the child's mouth. (Maybe I've not been gawping hard enough like these freaks who are so appalled.)

What you actually see when a baby is breast-feeding is . . . the back of their fucking head. And if you're disgusted by the back of a baby's head, you should see what comes out of their ass.

The strange thing is that it seems to be both men and women who have a problem with it, but again, who are they? Who are these women who are so delicate that the possibility of seeing a breast will make them keel over. . . . And who are these men who are so sheltered that seeing an uncloaked nipple might cause them to have an instantaneous stroke (and not the good kind).

It's odd. . . . These are people disgusted by a child having its dinner . . . usually while they are eating their own . . . really . . . what is so terrifying about the possibility of glimpsing an areola while simultaneously eating soup?

The ironic thing is that, if I'm describing you, you're probably the biggest tit in the restaurant. And you'll no doubt be the same jerk tutting when the baby cries because it is hungry.

So why am I banging on about this now?

We've just been for a pub meal and the couple across from us clearly had a problem with Lyns breast-feeding . . . (they used the international language of dickheads: i.e., "eye-rolling"). This is my first experience of the open hostility toward breast-feeding (I genuinely thought it was a myth).

So . . . I didn't say anything, but to piss them off I did take my shirt off and ate the rest of my chicken dinner topless. (And after overindulging over Christmas, I've developed quite a decent rack.)

Anyway . . . I'm pleased to report a small victory: they did leave without dessert, and Mr. Dickhead didn't even finish his pint.

That said, it did backfire a bit . . . I burnt one of my man-tits with a bit of Yorkshire pudding gravy and the sight of my white, pasty body put Lyns right off of her cheese and broccoli bake.

. . . Still, as they pissed off out the door, shaking their empty heads, it did feel like a moment of sisterhood.

Now, it's fair to say that this could have been an isolated incident. And it has been pointed out to me that maybe I was being oversensitive or protective or paranoid and maybe this was all in our heads. But we have come across similar reactions quite a few times since.

Besides, the online response to this post was bizarre and revealed that this sort of low-level disgust is being repeated in public places across the world.

The comments and messages I received were full of anecdotes about passive and overt hostility toward breast-feeding mothers. And if you think that all the women who got in touch were paranoid or fabricating incidents, what was far more revealing were the comments from those who were themselves anti-breast-feeding. These comments showed that these weirdos really do exist and in numbers. And when you read their comments, the level of "crazy" hits a new level. Like, level 10 crazy . . . which is Lady Gaga firing Charlie Sheen out of a custard cannon crazy.

Here's an example of the comments I received in response to the "Breast-feeding and the Weirdos" blog post:

Typical liberal bullshit. Why are these feminazis so desperate to show the world they're [sic] tits. I don't want to see it my family don't want to see it. Cover em up.

Mmm, bigoted, dim, weird, but not super crazy. Fair enough, what about this:

So, I should be allowed to let my balls hang out of my zipper and air out. They are not sexual and are storage tanks too. Another fine example of women wanting to be supreme instead of equal.

Or how about this:

How would men walking around with their penis at the ready for a pee be judged. This is normal in the animal and uncivilized world too but you men try it and see what's said.

See? Nuts. It was one thing to realize that some people can't cope with the sight of a nipple, but I had turned over a rock. And beneath it was a whole subculture of odd objectees who seemed to have a bizarre sexualized confusion about the whole thing. These were not the only comments I received that promoted the idea that breasts should be treated the same as cocks and/or balls, and should remain covered up for the sake of public decency.

To be honest, I didn't reply to many of these sorts of comments. I've found it's best not to engage with people that unstable. (There's always a chance that, the next thing you know, they're standing in your back garden drooling into the shrubbery.) But, since it's unlikely any of them can read long sentences, I'll say this:

It's just weird to think of breasts as solely sexual objects. I'm a heterosexual man who really likes breasts. But I'm also aware that their primary purpose is not for me to juggle two-handed while shouting "waahey!" at every opportunity. Their primary purpose is food. And, as a reasonably well-balanced adult, I'm able to see boobs as both sexual objects and as a source of nourishment for a child. I'm able to think contextually. After all, certain appendages of the body change in context. So a penis is something you urinate out of until you start waving it around at a bus stop, or, in a more appropriate example, your ass is something you defecate from until you start talking out of it.

I've dedicated a lot of time to arguing about this subject in the past year. But it seems the old saying holds true: You can't educate pork. And, rather than waste any more breath, I figured it's time to try to put an end to this debate. So I came up with this simple multiple-choice questionnaire that allows you to check whether you're in the wrong about this subject:

When you see a woman breast-feeding, do you think?:

A: What a lovely sight, a woman feeding her baby the way nature intended.

B: There's a baby having its dinner.

C: That's disgusting, it shouldn't be allowed, now I have to go home and clean my eyeballs, I've literally shit my pants I'm so appalled etc.

ANSWER: If you answered mainly Cs, you're a c'nt.

WEANING

Whether you choose to bottle-feed, brave the high weirdness of breast-feeding, combination-feed, or allow your baby to suckle from a friendly goat, sooner or later all babies must move on to solid foods. Otherwise you become one of those mothers still feeding her teenager with a nipple through the school gates. (As much as I'm against judging anyone for the decisions they make about breast-feeding, once your child is old enough to get milk froth in his mustache, it may be time to consider moving on.)

In medieval times, making the transition from milk to solid foods was regarded as quite a big deal. In a time of high infant mortality, it was thought of as an important milestone and taken really seriously. In the most serious book of all time, the Bible, it says that everyone who lives on milk is "unskilled in the word," whereas "solid food is for the mature, for those who have the power to distinguish between good and evil."

It seems a bit extreme to suggest that unless you get your tot onto chicken fingers sharpish, he won't be able to distinguish between good and evil. But if a book with talking animals, a man who lived in a whale, and a chatty bush says it's super important, then it's probably best to take it seriously.

Certainly, there is a lot of serious expert advice about weaning and when to start. The advice recommends after six months. But we were sure that Charlie was ready for proper food earlier because he'd started wanting extra milk and chewing on his fist like it was a burger. We figured that when your baby is starting to cannibalize himself, he's probably ready for a cookie. In fact, as it turns out, these aren't signs of being ready for food at all. They are false alarms and just stuff that babies do. One of the main signs that babies actually are ready is when they become really curious about what you are eating, so that's what we started to keep an eye out for. At around seven months, Charlie was more than curious. One night I was eating a pizza after getting home late from work, and he just looked at me mesmerized each time I lifted a slice to my mouth. And, as I finished the last piece, he stared hard at me as if to say: "I swear to God, if there isn't another slice in that box for me, I'm going to smash the place up." He was ready.

We were understandably worried about moving Charlie to solid foods. Just when we'd got him used to liquids, he was going to have to tackle something chokey. It all seemed something of a leap, like removing the training wheels from a kid's bike and making him ride it on a highway. There is, of course, a transition phase whereby the solid food is actually about as solid as nursing-home soup. But there does come that moment when you add to the spoon a bit of rice or a piece of pasta. And, although these more substantial bits of food are so cautiously small as to be barely visible to the human eye, it is a heart-stopping moment to see if your baby will swallow. They do. It's fine. Choking is really rare.

As well as the persistent, common fear of choking, we were also concerned about allergies. Apparently, these things can be passed down the generations, and as a kid I was allergic to a variety of foods. When I was about Charlie's age, I had a reaction to yellow food coloring and ballooned up like a puffer fish. I had to be rolled to the hospital for treatment for anaphylactic shock. "You looked like a cute little Fatty Arbuckle," my mom tells me. "I nearly died," I remind her. "A cute little Fatty Fatty Arbuckle," she persists as she pinches my forty-year-old cheeks. Unbelievable.

Thankfully, it appears I didn't pass on my bad allergy genes, and Charlie has had no problem tolerating the smush we serve up.

In fact, once we'd gotten past our own fears, weaning Charlie was incredibly straightforward. I know a lot of parents have a hard time at this transitional stage, but I guess we were just really lucky, and Charlie took to food like a duck to bread.

There were very few foods he disliked. One of the leaflets we read said that it is important to try your baby on different types of food to see what she likes and what she dislikes. It said that you should learn to read your baby's face, as it can be difficult to tell. Not really. In my limited experience, if babies like a food, their faces light up and their mouths open like yawny hippos. If they don't like it, they contort their faces like they've just been fed mashed-up rat's anus. There's not a great deal of room for confusion.

But even if you are lucky enough to have a baby who will eat any old crap, it's important to remember that there are certain foods to avoid. Obviously, it's going to be a while before junior can tuck into a rib-eye or whatever, but apparently there are other foods that are no good.

BAD FOOD, GOOD FOOD

We are told repeatedly that if we are not suitably cautious about the stuff we feed our babies, they will overdose on salt and sugar and grow into child blimps. Who, by the time they're six, will need one of those courtesy electric mobility scooters they provide at shopping centers. Gone are the days when you can just blast some SpaghettiOs in a microwave and consider yourself a good parent. That shit's deadly.

So, what to feed them? After a brief bit of research on the new UK moms' forum Netmums, I uncovered a pretty clear rule: basically, the more painfully hipster and middle-class the food is, the better.

According to a netmums.com weaning guide, things like avocado, breadsticks, quinoa, and tofu are all great options. (If you can't remember the full list, it's pretty much anything from Whole Foods.)

Handily, the same list cautions against feeding your baby certain staple foods that can be found in "every" family's food cupboard. Things like goat's milk, Stilton, honey, and, of course, shark or marlin.

Well, I for one am glad I came across this list before making Charlie my signature dish of Cheesy Honeyed Shark.

It could be argued that these lists aren't very inclusive and that they contain items that don't necessarily apply to normal people's weekly shopping. Also, these lists are supposed to encourage healthy eating in babies and tackle childhood obesity. But poorer areas tend to be the ones suffering most from childhood obesity—and, I'll be absolutely honest, on the fairly low-income housing estate where I grew up, avocado, hummus, and the finest blue cheeses weren't that big on the teatime menu.

Poorer families are feeding their kids on a budget, not inviting Heston Blumenthal to stop by for a tasting menu. What's wrong with these lists being a bit more relevant: crackers instead of breadsticks, rice rather than quinoa, and the rancid rubber from an old flip-flop instead of tofu? Just recommending that everybody should try to cut down on the Stilton suggests that the experts may be a tad out of touch.

One of the other things that we are discouraged from feeding to our young is anything that is packaged: anything that comes in a packet, a can, or a jar. Try producing a pouch of food in a group of organics-obsessed parents and wait for the glances of disapproval, as though you're about to spoon-feed your baby sulfur.

What parents are supposed to do is cook and puree all the baby's food from scratch. Preferably having picked the vegetables themselves, naked and by moonlight, thanking Gaia, the Mother Earth, for her blessings and sacrifice.

The problem with this is our old enemy: time. It takes longer than you think to chop vegetables, steam or boil them, and then blend them to a puree (and then clean up the mess afterward). And the most disheartening thing is how little food you end up with. You can amass a pile of vegetables the size of a car, but once they are steamed and pureed you wind up with three tiny jars of food and are left scratching your head wondering where the fuck it all went. You also now have a washing-up pile the size of K2.

So jars or pouches of baby food are sometimes a godsend. Particularly when you're away from home and you don't happen to have your pile of fresh vegetables, fresh chicken, range, knife, steamer, and blender on hand. I know there are many weaning gurus who are militantly against anything that comes in a pouch, and it's probably true to say that not all baby food is created equal. And maybe a lot of it doesn't have the same nutrients as fresh food. But I'd wager it's come a long way since the baby food we used to eat as kids, which was one part salt to two parts sugar and had enough food coloring in it to make your shit glow.

So if Charlie eats from a pouch sometimes, I don't think his hair's going to fall out or he's going to be struck down with scurvy. I think he'll be fine.

Besides, after about a year, supposedly, this all gets a bit easier, because at that point they should start eating the same as you. The problem is that for the past year, you haven't really eaten. In fact, it's a wonder we're all still alive.

The last meal we had before Charlie was born was a grand Sunday lunch. A towering plate of roast beef and vegetables, with all the trimmings. The last Sunday lunch we had, as I write this, was a peanut butter sandwich. I say sandwich. Actually, we had no bread, so me and Lyns just sat there side by side, spooning the peanut butter into our mouths with our bare hands like emaciated bears that had stumbled across a discarded jar.

Charlie actually eats like a king, but the meals that we manage are invariably takeout. It's to be hoped that Charlie doesn't start to eat the same as us, since we subsist on horrendously unhealthy Chinese food, Indian, and fish and chips. I've never eaten particularly well, but, since having Charlie, we eat like we're trying to commit suicide by MSG. My cholesterol level has gone up to 7.6 (about 290 on the American scale), which means, in layman's terms, I am more pork rind than human. Like I said, it's amazing we're still alive. The plan is to make our own diets healthier before we share the same food with Charlie. But I think we're going to have to do it gradually. At this stage, my body couldn't take moving rapidly to a diet that included a fruit or a vegetable. I fear it would reject the goodness, I'd go into shock, and my insides would burst.

TO BATTLE

Of course, to look at any baby after she's just eaten, you'd think that there is no way that any of the food has actually made it into her mouth, let alone her stomach. Charlie is no different: whatever food he eats, he ends the meal coated in it. Actually, he doesn't look like he's been eating at all: he looks more like his meal just exploded in front of him before he could start.

Apparently, this is a good sign. From what I've seen, all kids, up to the age of three, finish every meal looking like they've been around the back of the house and in the garbage cans. One of the defining characteristics of thriving, happy babies is that they are covered in yogurt, have styled their hair with baked-bean juice, and have jammed their ears up with squished fruit.

So, there are two main approaches to baby feeding:

Baby-led weaning and spoon-led weaning
At this stage, we are told that babies are "exploring" their food. While it would be nice if they ate some of it while they were at it, all the advice encourages this exploration. And baby-led weaning really encourages babies to explore their food with their hands.

Which is all well and good, but the experts don't give a great deal of advice about how to avoid the surrounding area looking like the Battle of Little Bighorn has just been reenacted using a wedding buffet.

The bib is the most useless piece of clothing invented since those floor-dusting shoes you can get for cats. It protects the six inches below a baby's chin but does nothing about you, your furniture, or the rest of the room—the area best thought of as a kind of "blast radius." I've seen suggestions that it is best to put down some newspapers, and that's not a bad idea for protecting the floor. But if your little one is anything like Charlie, you would need to deck out the entire room in plastic sheeting, like TV serial killer Dexter just before he's about to brutally murder one of his victims. Charlie's range is prodigious. After one particularly lively meal of pasta, I was peeling spaghetti off the TV and the patio doors . . . which are in different rooms. Even when we thought we'd got it all cleared up, we were sitting watching television a few days later and smelled burning, which turned out to be a piece of pasta stuck dangling from a lightbulb. (I even went to work the following day and found some in my pocket.) Pasta, though, is an easy thing to clean up by comparison with some of the other substances that form a baby's diet. According to *New Scientist*, the hardest substance known to man is the diamondlike "wurtzite boron nitride," but it's pretty clear that they never tested mashed-up Weetabix that has been allowed to dry on a window. While it's still wet, a wet wipe will easily get rid of it; when it's dry, you can burn your way through an angle grinder just trying to make a dent in it. If you are going to try baby-led weaning, my advice is to get a dog. Our Jack Russell, Eddie, has put on fifteen pounds in the last few months minesweeping the house for lost food. And if he keeps licking the Weetabix stuck to the window, that could be gone in a matter of years.

Spoon-led weaning provides its own challenges. While it's marginally less messy, it's still advisable to dress in full overalls and goggles when feeding anything sloppy—which at this age is everything.

Because you are spoon-feeding your baby, it is better in one respect, in that you can gauge how much your child is actually ingesting. You don't have to just wander around the room, trying to calculate what didn't make it into her mouth. You can measure it spoon by spoon. You can also encourage her to eat using tried and tested methods such as pretending that the spoon is a train or an airplane. (It's ridiculous how babies will clamp their mouths shut for a spoonful of food but will open up if you can convince them that it's actually a form of transportation.)

Of course, it's not that straightforward. As much as Charlie enjoys his food, he enjoys much more the fun of waiting until a full spoon is almost delivered to his mouth before swatting it away at the last minute. This creates delightful abstract art up the back of the sofa or across the walls. If you put the bowl too close to Charlie, he will tip that over as well. Deliberately. Feeding him is like being bullied in a prison cafeteria. You're just minding your own business, and he just tips the lot over deliberately for no reason: "Clean that shit up, bitch, this is my wing."

So spoon-feeding is by no means a clean option. And there is one extremely important rule: never hand over control of the spoon.

Giving Charlie power over the spoon is like weaponizing him. Having food on the spoon gives him the ability to launch that food farther. When he doesn't have food on the spoon, he jabs it into his own eye or rams it down his throat like he's a sword swallower. Try to get it away from him, and it's back to "prison rules"—he wields it like a shank in a jailhouse dustup. He drums with it, conducts an invisible orchestra with it, and tries to force it into his nose. He does everything with it but use it to eat. *Never* relinquish the spoon. (Until you have to, obviously. You don't want to get your child to eighteen and still be sitting next to him in the dining hall, spooning his food in with an encouraging "choo-choo.")

SCREW THE MESS

I love watching Charlie eat. Screw the mess.

The way he flings his food around, makes fart noises as he raspberries, hiccups, and burps his way through his meal. I love his facial expressions when he loves something and love them even more when it's something he detests. I love the way he washes his face in his food and the wild-armed abandon with which he can approach a single bean or a mashed-up banana.

It seems a shame that we are teaching him to lose that enjoyment. And maybe we are the ones who should be learning something instead.

As adults, we take the whole food thing way too seriously. The pathetic way we section off our potatoes from our carrots, and divide our courses into savory and sweet, and eat them in the right order and with the appropriate cutlery and with our mouths closed. It's sad.

I have lost count of the number of times I have sat and watched an episode of *MasterChef* and, as the melodramatic music reached a crescendo, thought: *For fuck's sake, it's not the Cuban missile crisis, it's a fucking shepherd's pie.*

Where did this seriousness about food come from? What happened to the pure enjoyment of food that we see when a baby eats well?

I'm not saying that adults should return to eating soup with their fingers and throwing gravy at the walls when they are having a pub lunch (or maybe I am). What I am saying is that we have lost the true joy of food. And if we apply that seriousness to children and babies (even with the best of intentions), maybe we are spoiling something beautifully childish.

So I think we're going to let Charlie explore his food for as long as he likes, and fling it around until he decides not to. Maybe we'll let him eat the occasional thing not on the officially sanctioned list of foods. Maybe not everything he eats will be organic. Maybe sometimes it will be from a pouch or a jar and have too much sugar in it.

And maybe when he's a little older and he turns to me one day and says, "Dad, I really don't like these vegetables," maybe one time I'll say:

"You know what, Charlie boy? Me neither. . . . Fuck it, let's just have pie."

6

OUTSIDE

A while ago I was on holiday and, while impressively drunk, was talked by a couple of mates into doing a parachute jump. The following day, just before we were due to board this shitty little plane, I was nervously filling out a disclaimer form when I noticed the small print: it said that in the event of something going wrong, we were insured "third party." I asked the Australian guy running the place what that meant, and he said, "Mate, that means if your 'chute doesn't open and you slam into a shed . . . well . . . the shed's covered."

The way I felt at that moment is the same as I feel today as we are about to go outside for the first time with Charlie . . . like we're about to jump out of a plane from twenty thousand feet. Home has become a safe place and leaving that safety is daunting. I know we'll probably be fine . . . but I can't shake the feeling that this is a real leap, and that there's a chance that we will panic, we'll get into a flat spin, our parachute will fail to open properly, and we'll slam into the side of a shed.

We're only going to IKEA.

OUTSIDE

On August 23, 1973, during a robbery, three women and one man were taken hostage in one of the largest banks in Stockholm. They were then held captive for several days by two ex-convicts. The hostages were sleep-deprived, hungry, and confused. But, in this state, something strange happened: they began to identify with the bank robbers, even developing affection for them. (Two of the women eventually got engaged to their captors.)

Psychologists who studied this phenomenon discovered that this was a common response to being held hostage. So much so that, following the case, they gave the condition a name: they called it Stockholm syndrome. It had certain characteristics:

- Perceived inability to escape.
- Isolation from perspectives other than those of the captor.
- The captive's perception of small kindnesses from the captor within a context of terror.

I've not come across many better descriptions of being a new parent.

With this in mind, after a while it's important to go outside for some fresh air and to meet other people—if only to be sure that you've actually bonded with your baby and you are not just suffering from Stockholm syndrome and identifying with your captor.

And so, wish us luck as we go blinking into the sunlight for the first time. Outside: that place where we used to go before having a baby. A mythical, foreign place, of drinks and meals and other people.

Unwashed, unkempt, and cripplingly sleep-deprived, we look like we've spent the last decade chained to a radiator in Beirut. But we are determined to leave the comfort of our nest, committed to living a life outside of four walls, eager to proudly venture, forthright in stride, in th—

Oh, for fuck's sake . . . we've forgotten something.

MOBILIZE

The amount of stuff required to keep a baby alive away from home is breathtaking. Napoleon took slightly less stuff to invade Russia than you now need to nip to the shops: wipes, diapers, diaper bags, toys, stroller, stroller cover, car seat, blankets, hat, clothes, extra clothes, extra emergency clothes, phone, phone charger, spit-up cloths, bibs, the slowly dissipating will to live.

I've heard stories about people having to turn around and go back home for the baby. And I can believe it. This is a mobilization rather than an exit. Before Charlie, my preparations for leaving the house consisted of grabbing a Kit Kat and remembering to wear pants. But with a baby in tow, the entire contents of our house must now be emptied into the car. Or, if we're venturing out on foot, into the tiny basket that hangs like a camel's ball-sack from the bottom of our baby's stroller.

THE "STROLLER"

So let's assume, for our first trip, that we are venturing out into the world on foot. The most vital piece of equipment for this sort of expedition is what we British call the pram.* The pushchair. Or, as marketing bastards deceptively rebranded it when we weren't looking:

---

*I don't know why Americans don't use the word *pram*. It's short for "the Perambulator"—which sounds like a really shit wrestler, but was actually the name of an early stroller patented by an American guy called Charles Burton. Apparently, he was struck by the fact that: "Carrying a heavy child in the arms . . . is not only a wearisome occupation, but often one which . . . is the cause of serious injuries." Which is nineteenth-century speak for: "This kid weighs a ton and keeps kicking me in the bollocks."

the stroller. (Because, in marketing land, new parents "stroll." Rather than tear-ass around the place insanely, using their stroller like a chariot in *Ben-Hur*, as they try to get a week's tasks done in the fifteen-minute window while their little one is sleeping.)

I used to think that a stroller was just a way of attaching wheels to your child. He can't walk, you can't carry him all the time, so what could be simpler than a straightforward piece of equipment that has somewhere for a baby to sit, four wheels, and a pushing handle? I thought that a stroller was essentially a padded wheelbarrow. After spending six months wheeling 472 different varieties up and down the aisles of Babies"R"Us, I realize I was wrong. There are countless different types, all with dopey lifestyle-y names like The Windsor and Zest. Far from simple, these things are some of the most unnecessarily complex and complicated appliances ever created by humankind. And the companies that manufacture and sell them make the process of buying one all the more confusing with their bullshit.

Here are two different descriptions:

1. The frame is an ergonomically designed carbon fiber chassis with aluminum alloy wheels and a four-wheel independent suspension, to handle the toughest terrain. The underside is coated in heat-resistant material that helps to maintain temperature.

2. The lightweight frame is made of aluminum alloy and carbon composites, aluminum wheels are mounted on a rocker-boogie suspension so that the wheels remain on the ground over rough terrain. Each front and rear wheel can be individually steered allowing for 360-degree turns.

So, example number one is a manufacturer's description of the stroller we bought.

Example number two is NASA's description of the Mars Rover vehicle *Curiosity*.

You see what I mean about unnecessarily complicated bullshit? Based on these two descriptions alone, I couldn't tell you which is a stroller and which is a $2.5 billion engineering project to visit and collect data from the Red Planet.

(In fact, if I'd ordered online, I could have ordered the wrong one. But for the lack of a $2.5 billion limit on my Visa card, we could easily have found ourselves pushing Charlie around Costco in an interplanetary research robot.)

THE DEATH STROLLER 1000

In fairness to the lady who sold us our stroller, she did her best to simplify the attributes of each model we looked at. Janet explained that "carbon fiber chassis" just meant that it was light, "enhanced steel frame" meant that it was tough, and so on. But, as a salesperson, Janet was also keen to stress the added value of the more expensive models.

(My responses were in my head, by the way):

Janet: "This particular model has independent suspension and all-weather and -terrain wheels."

That's great, but we want to be able to take him to IKEA, not up Kilimanjaro.

Janet: "This particular model is the same one used by Prince William and Kate for Prince George."

I'll be honest, Janet, I don't give a shit if the Pope pushed Jesus around in it. It's expensive. Even if it came dipped in gold, with diamond handles, and fired a confetti cannon every time the baby crapped, it would be expensive.

Janet: "This particular model has a UPF 50+ UV sun canopy."

This is England.

Janet: "This particular model has a retractable sun parasol."
This is England.

Janet: "This particular model has a mosquito net."
Janet? You do know this is England, right? So far, I'm being sold the perfect vehicle to take a baby up a mountain, across a desert, and through a malarial swamp.

Janet: "This particular model has a lifetime guarantee."
Great . . . if we lose a wheel when we're pushing Charlie around in his forties, we'll be sure to cash that in.

Janet: "This particular model comes with an easy three-stage folding mechanism."
Okay, sorry, Janet, but no, it doesn't. You've just spent fifteen minutes with a vein popping on the side of your head trying to collapse the thing, and you work here.

Finally, Janet, with something of a flourish, pointed out the remaining attributes of this top-of-the-line, all-singing, all-dancing kid barrow:

Janet: "This particular model also has leatherette trim, a plastic hook for a shopping bag, and a cup holder."
. . . A cup holder?

I wasn't impressed at the time, and I am even less so now. I have no idea who designs strollers, but I'm pretty sure that any of us who have shoved one around, for the shortest amount of time, could come up with better features than a cup holder . . . and I'm not talking about leatherette trim.

These things should be customized, like the cars in *Mad Max*, with flamethrowers and armor: people wandering toward you with their heads buried in their cell phone screens should be bouncing off the thing. Or chewed under its wheels. And pity the poor bastard who gets in the way of, or doesn't open the door for, a mom pushing the Death Stroller 1000 while frantically looking for a baby-changing room. He wouldn't stand a chance.

While we're at it, the thing should be fitted with spiked monster-truck wheels and a klaxon car horn, or better still, speakers blaring Norwegian death metal or "Highway to the Danger Zone." And screw a cup holder—what about a bar shelf along the handle or a sidecar for a keg? This thing could be fucking awesome.

On a more practical level: forget the plastic hook. The basket underneath should be the size of a house. The whole thing should be weighted to the front so that no matter how many bags you hang from the handle, you don't tip the baby upside down. The canopy should absorb sound and have built-in GPS to the nearest Walgreens. It should have a wet-wipe dispenser, be self-cleaning, and have an alarm that goes off to remind you that you've put an entire box of Krispy Kremes in the bottom of your stroller before you collapse it to put it in the car and turn your donuts into a custardy abomination.

. . . But back to Janet.

And here we were, being told that this "particular model" was great, simply because it had a plastic holder where we could put a can of soda.

As I daydreamed about the Death Stroller 1000, Janet concluded her sales pitch about this one particularly expensive stroller (it was called The Inspire, or some markety bollocks like that). We had listened for more than half an hour as she demonstrated and explained the many attributes of this "beautiful stroller." And I distinctly remember chuckling to myself as she told us the total price. I thought: *This woman must think we're idiots; that* we *are the ones born yesterday.*

I smiled and threw Lyns a sideways glance, a brief knowing look to convey how ridiculous it was that Janet could think us so dumb.

I waited for a glance of agreement back, but in return Lyns gave me a look that said: "This is the one."

. . . And so I handed over the best part of a month's salary, and died a little inside.

Incidentally, it would ordinarily be me who displayed the kind of gullibility required to buy an $800 chair with four wheels. I once spent our last twenty bucks on a limited-edition Boba Fett voice-changing helmet. So this whole experience was a bit of a role reversal. But Lyndsay was already in love before Charlie was even born. A love I didn't really discover until he crash-landed. And the only way to convey that love, without him being there to care for and hold, was to buy him shit. And not just any old shit, but the best of shit. It isn't reasonable and it isn't sane, but Lyndsay convinced me with a pat of her belly that we needed to spend more than we could afford to get the perfect stroller. And, without a model that had flamethrowers attached to it, this was as good as it got.

Actually, as it turned out, the one we chose was quite a good buy. Janet was a lying harpy, though. The all-terrain stuff was bullshit: it was all-terrain only so long as that terrain wasn't mud, sand, grass, ice, snow, decking, gravel, slightly cracked pavement, or somewhat rough tarmac.

Also, it turned out that Wills and Kate did not own the same stroller as us. I checked: according to the papers, they bought one for about $23,000, so unless we got a fairly hefty discount on ours (or the future heir to the throne got properly shafted by Janet), it wasn't the same one.

And the claim that it had an "easy three-stage folding mechanism" was actually true, but only in those rare circumstances when you've got both hands free. With just one hand free, you have to fight the fucking thing, parking lot rules, until it gets tired. (If you're really lucky, it's less than an hour of hand-to-stroller combat before the bastard thing begrudgingly surrenders and pops open.)

But, all that said, The Inspire was comfy and it was warm and Charlie seemed to like it.

Until he didn't.

STROLLER WARS

Babies reach an age when they don't want to be in the stroller all the time. I'm guessing they get sick to death of always being at balls level and want a different perspective. The problem is that this desire to be free comes before their ability to walk. So, them not being in the stroller means you have to carry them around all the time like an idiot farm boy with a sack of potatoes. The good news is that, if you decide that they should stay in the stroller, babies don't have the intellect to do anything about it. Their brains aren't fully formed, they can't compete with your superior intelligence, and therefore they can't possibly come up with any way of avoiding it.

Only joking. Of course they can. In fact, they've got two really effective ways of avoiding it.

Technique 1
The first way a baby avoids being placed in his stroller is by refusing to bend. If a baby decides that the stroller is not where he wants to be, he can and will arch his back and stiffen every muscle in his body

until he is about as compliant as a block of wood and it is impossible to make him fold or flex or comply. It doesn't matter how strong you are, whether you're built like Betty White or The Rock; all parents are helpless against this previously unseen power of rigor mortis. It's not just a battle of strength, it's a battle of awkwardness. It's kind of like trying to put skis into a bread bin. The move is brilliant, really. A simple alternative to fight-or-flight and an awesome way of avoiding pretty much anything you don't want to do. The next time I'm at work and I'm asked to do something I don't want to do, I'm going to try it:

"Matt, could you just take a look at the figures for the last quarter."

"Fuck you, Carl" . . . as I stiffen my entire body and fall to the ground and lie there like a plank.

Nothing anyone can do. Ingenious.

Technique 2

If somehow, by speed or by distraction, you successfully origami-fold your baby into her stroller, she still has another tried and tested method of avoiding confinement.

When threatened, Malaysian ants and French Guianese termites will react by exploding. These things literally blow themselves up, and babies have a similar "nuclear option" at their disposal. It is a method of defense that babies will use in all manner of scenarios, precisely because it is so effective. In layman's terms: they will lose their fucking minds. Kick, bite, wrestle, claw, and scream hysterically until everybody within fifteen feet feels like their face is going to burst. And as you notice that bystanders, with blood pouring from their ears, are falling to the ground, begging God for it to stop, you concede. You give in. You lose. You take your baby back into your arms and she is instantly calm, instantly quiet, and you say to yourself, *Okay . . . but next time . . .*

But in that same moment, unbeknownst to you, neurons are firing in your little one's tiny brain. Neural pathways are being explored and connections being made, never to be broken. And those tiny sparks in new gray matter amount to a discovered knowledge. A knowledge that is expressed in the slightest of smiles, as your baby now sits contentedly in your arms:

"I fucking own you."

CARRIER

So the alternative to the stroller is to just carry your baby around all the time. The problem is that babies weigh anything between ten and twenty-five pounds. Which is the same as carrying around a pet bag of cement. Also, a bag of cement is a dead weight; it doesn't move. A baby, on the other hand, likes to vogue in your arms, striking a different pose every fifteen seconds. Forcing you to constantly adjust your arms or else drop him on his ungrateful, awkward head. This is okay for a maximum of fifteen minutes, but any longer and it feels like you no longer have bones in your arms and your spine is being torn out by Predator and shown to the moonlight.

The solution to this problem is a simple one: a carrier. Which is kind of like a big wearable holster for your baby.

I refused to buy one of these. If I'm honest, I associated them with those really "try hard" husbands who "experienced" birth with their partners and enjoy the feel of a good corduroy. I felt like wearing one was maybe a short step away from strapping on a pair of fake lactating boobs and getting the baby to sleep by playing acoustic guitar. I also just thought that on a man they looked a bit odd. I could see that women with their newborns looked adorable in them. But for some reason, whenever I'd seen a man wearing one I just thought he looked a bit like an awkward man/kangaroo hybrid (a "mangaroo"), and that the baby hanging from his chest looked like the mutant Kuato from the original *Total Recall* (which is an obscure reference but dead accurate if you can be bothered to Google it).

Lyns already had a sling that she used all the time, and if Charlie didn't want to be in his stroller when we were all together, he was usually in that. But when it was just me and Charlie, carting him around in my arms everywhere was brutal. Eventually, after considering it for a long time, I caved and ordered a carrier. (I figured if I was ever going to try it, there was no point in continuing to put it off. Or by the time I got around to it, Charlie would be a teenager, and as he sat in it, his feet would be touching the floor. It would just look like he was carrying an old man around in a rucksack.)

When it arrived, it was shit. It was all plastic clips and straps and had an uncomfortably rigid back support. It looked like a cross between a straitjacket and the kind of industrial, no-nonsense bra that a woman who could beat the living shit out of you would wear.

What it looked like wasn't the only issue. After a week or so, I reviewed it on Amazon. Without reprinting the whole thing, these were my main concerns:

- Trying to get it on feels like you're being sexually assaulted by a set of bagpipes.
- It says in the instructions that it's designed so that you feel a real bond with your baby . . . when I wear it, I feel like I'm doing a tandem skydive with Verne Troyer.
- The baby sits at exactly the right height to reverse head-butt you in the chin, but low enough to repeatedly kick you in the testicles.

Now, you'd be forgiven for thinking from these excerpts that this was a negative review. But in fact I still gave it four stars—for the simple reason that Charlie absolutely loves it. He was suddenly four feet taller and enjoying striding around the place like he was King Kong. (After spending his first few months on the planet as a two-foot-tall weakling, climbing into his carrier he must have felt like Sigourney Weaver at the end of *Aliens* when she gets into that big forklift suit thing and turns dead hard.) Seeing the look of joy on his face as we took our first walk was great. But this was tempered somewhat by the horrifying realization that there was no way this boy was going back in his stroller.

After wearing the carrier for a matter of minutes, I did try to put him back into his stroller, and he just looked at me: "Er, Dad, I ain't getting in that, strollers are for dicks."

So after I posted the carrier review I was inundated with suggestions and recommendations for other models that were less testicularly aggressive. And eventually I found one that actually works pretty well, is quite comfortable, and, when trying to get it on, feels a bit less like being molested by a sea monster. Now I wear it all the time, and not just because it spares my aching arms and back: it also feels good to share a perspective with Charlie and experience the world from the same angle for a while.

And if I look like a mangaroo or one of those "try hard" dads I was so unfair about, then fuck it, there are worse things to be.

BY CAR

Visiting the outside world on foot can be complicated, so you might want to take your first excursion by car.

One of the main problems with traveling around by car is that, to begin with, it's pretty slow going. For the first few months I drove everywhere at walking pace. I was ludicrously cautious when Charlie was in the back. But it can't be helped; with such a fragile creature on board, you feel like you're hurtling along at light speed only to look down and discover that you've topped out at sixteen miles an hour and a line of traffic is building behind you—a line of traffic that includes tractors, trailers, and a funeral procession driving right up your ass, with the bereaved relatives hanging out of the hearse windows shouting: "Fucking today, grandma!"

(In fact, an aggressive-looking old guy with a bushy gray beard actually had a go at me for driving too slowly, a point he made by driving within a millimeter of my back bumper and giving me the universal "wanker" gesture. I'm not a road-ragey kind of person, but when we pulled up at the lights I wound down my passenger window and calmly pointed out that I was obeying the speed limit and that he should practice more caution. I think my exact words were: "Fuck off, Dumbledore."

Satisfied that I'd won that particular argument, I pressed the electric button to put the window back up and pressed the wrong one. Making the back window go down. And, because that back window now had a sun blind suctioned to it, the entire blind was dragged into the door of the car with a horrific grinding noise. It's still in there somewhere. I was alongside the same guy at the next set of lights and had to face forward for the longest forty seconds of my life, as all I could see out of the corner of my eye was Albus Dumbledore pissing his pants laughing and offering the same universal gesture he'd offered a few moments before.)

The problem with driving is that you suddenly see danger everywhere; every roundabout and set of traffic lights has a potential for disaster, and highways become a kind of dystopian death-race. It can be terrifying. The ridiculous thing is that the real problem is inside your own car. When you're driving along, there is no greater danger than you. Constantly checking your mirror to be sure that the baby hasn't chewed through his harness and escaped. Or, worse, turning around persistently to comfort him as he screeches about something universe-shakingly important like a dropped raisin.

The distraction of a baby being in the car is far greater than the use of a cell phone or fiddling with the radio. It's a bit like being carjacked, being made to drive with a gun to your head. Or, more accurately, it's like you've picked up a psychotic hitchhiker who is sitting there in the backseat behaving normally for now, but could go mental at any second.

In fact, if they really wanted to test the skill and dexterity of the modern NASCAR driver, they should fit a backseat in every car, and put a three-month-old baby in it. Six laps round the Daytona Speedway, and Dale Earnhardt Jr. would be pulling into the pit lane, frazzled and in tears, eating snot-covered chocolate, and insisting: "I can't do this anymore."

CAR SEAT

Car seats have come a long way since they were first invented in the 1930s. If you image-search pictures of the first versions, you'll be horrified. Modern car seats are engineered by the finest of scientific minds, whereas these early versions look like they were knocked together in the shed by your dad. Made out of metal and wood, they were nailed together as though the brief was to create something that in the event of a collision would collapse like an iron maiden. The makers of these things couldn't have been less safety-conscious if they had chosen to manufacture them out of broken bottles and bears' teeth. Not only were they phenomenally unsafe, but they look about as comfortable a place to sit as Jimmy Savile's lap.

In fairness, back then these things weren't designed for comfort or safety. They were just designed to keep the baby in place. To keep it from crawling around on the backseat as you barreled along smoking a ciggie on the way home from the local dive.

Is anyone else starting to wonder how babies of the past ever made it to adulthood? Health and safety for babies doesn't seem to have existed before the 1980s. Before that, safety concerns seem to have been restricted to making sure that if your baby got hold of a carving knife, he held the right end. In fact, now that I think of it, in every picture of me as a kid, I'm either playing in the road, cycling without a helmet, or hurtling toward certain death on a sled made of forklift truck pallets. I certainly didn't have a car seat. In fact, I vaguely remember spending most of my childhood arguing with my brother and sister about who'd be allowed to travel in the trunk.

Thankfully, safety and comfort were introduced into car seats by the 1990s, and the modern ones look as though they could survive reentry into the earth's atmosphere. They are padded, luxurious, reclining La-Z-Boys, based on the technology found in racing cars and designed to absorb the impact of any collision. Which is a great thing, especially since there are ten times as many cars on the road as when I was a kid and most of them go a lot faster than the shitty Morris Minor that was our family car (which could just about reach thirty miles an hour before it shook itself apart and caught fire).

As I said, the finest scientific minds were brought together to create this modern car seat. The problem was that you needed the finest scientific mind to install the thing in your car. Apparently, only a few years ago, 75 percent of all car seats were installed incorrectly, and it's not surprising. The seat belt of your car had to be threaded and looped, under and over, through baffling plastic catches, until the belt ran out of slack and you were still three inches short of actually clipping the thing in. Parents spent half the time concentrating on installing the seat and half the time fighting the demon on their shoulder that was whispering, "Fuck it, that'll do," reminding themselves that this was a matter of life and death, before they resorted to just duct-taping the baby to the rear headrest.

This is why the invention of Isofix is such a great thing. Isofix is a system of little metal bars hidden in the backseat of your car. The base of a modern car seat just clips onto these bars and you don't have to use the seat belt at all. It's genius. And it genuinely saves lives. Not least because after four hours of fighting to install the old seat-belt style, most parents wanted to lie down in the driveway and reverse the car over their own head.

Incidentally, our first car seat came as a package with the stroller we bought from Janet, and even though it was an Isofix design, it was with some relief that I noticed that there was an offer to have it installed in your car by in-store staff. *Thank God,* I thought, *I'm really shit at this sort of stuff and it's important that it's right.*

117

The problem with asking for the free installation service was that Janet kept banging on about how installing these new car seats was "idiot-proof" and that "a monkey could do it." So, despite Lyndsay quietly suggesting that we take advantage of the offer, in the end there was no way I could actually request the service. It would have been like declaring I was half a man.

I carted the box out to the car, concerned as to whether I was up to the job.

But on our drive home, part of me thought, maybe, just maybe, this could be a watershed moment.

I am not what you'd describe as a manly man. I have to get my father-in-law (a six-foot-four ex-steelworker) to come by just to put up a shelf. To make matters worse, the last time he did, when he asked me to hold the level for him, I said: "Ooh, that's cold." . . . He just looked at me with disgust. Like I said, I'm not a macho type.

But with this "idiot-proof" car seat installation came an opportunity, and something primal stirred within. This was an invitation to rise to a challenge. I thought, in just a few months' time I was going to be a father, a masculine role model, the man of the house, the head of the family, a hunting, gathering protector. It was time to step up and start doing this stuff.

I was man.

So I took the car seat home, unpacked it all with purpose, laid out the instructions carefully, studied them for a moment . . . and then phoned Lyndsay's dad and put the kettle on.

PUBLIC TRANSPORTATION

No. Just no.

. . .

Okay, fair enough. Not all of us have the option not to use public transportation. Some people don't drive, some people can't afford a car, some people live in a big city. And some people are masochists who want to fight their way onto a bus, packed with people desperate to avoid eye contact just so they don't have to give up their seat to passengers with one leg or a baby in their arms.

In fairness, in Britain we have a great reputation for courtesy, and on the whole I think that it's deserved. I just don't think that it applies on the X89 from Rotherham to Doncaster. This was the last journey I took on a bus with Charlie. It was packed with ignorant assholes and was driven by a depressive who (despite having a passenger standing up with a baby in his arms) drove his bus like a stagecoach being pursued by Apaches.

I was only on the X89 for fifteen minutes, but my fairly negative experience failed to be elevated by a group of aggressive teenagers, a daytime-drinking loon, and the haunting smell of takeout food and urine. This was the last time I took the bus with Charlie.

If you happen to be in London, the Tube is a better option. Generally speaking, the London Underground has always been a great way to get from A to B, have your wallet stolen, or get felt up by a stranger. But, at quieter times of day, it can also be a great way of getting around with your baby. If you can avoid the stations without elevators and with exits that are seven miles from where you get off, it is perfect. At rush hour, it's war.

Few allowances are made for a parent and baby during the London rush hour. Understandably so. If you've done a soul-shreddingly shitty job for the past ten hours, all you want to do is get home. (And I've done some jobs that were so shitty I would have pushed Gandhi onto the third rail if he threatened to delay my journey homeward.) So you need to be prepared to fight.

This is where I learned to wield our stroller like a mighty weapon. You may not have a Death Stroller 1000, but if you want to board a Tube at rush hour and you have a kid chariot, you need to be prepared to run up to the closing doors and ramrod the shit out of people's ankles to get aboard.

Once safely aboard, though, there remains a minefield of problems. Even without a baby, a packed Tube is not a particularly pleasant environment. It's a speeding capsule of sweat and closeness that the English ordinarily find horrifying. (If we wanted to be close to other people, we'd move to one of those touchy-feely countries like France or Italy.)

But with a stroller, you have never been more in the way. Whichever door you position yourself against will be on the side of the Tube that will open and close at every stop, to let the whole of Greater London get on and off. And while you're constantly trying to shift yourself to a place where you are less of an obstacle, you have to always be on the lookout for what your baby is up to. A couple of times I have looked down to discover Charlie methodically emptying the contents of some oblivious woman's handbag onto the floor. In fact, we disembarked at Covent Garden once with him clutching an eyeliner, a train ticket, and a packet of tissues. We still have no idea where he got them, but he presumably swiped them from someone else's unattended bag. I was a clueless Fagin to his Artful Dodger.

THE TRAIN

Traveling by train is very similar to traveling by the subway, and the same guiding principle exists: when it's quiet, it's great; when it's peak time, it's horrendous.

One of our first trips was on a train to London around Christmas, and it was completely full. The only available seats on the train were in the "quiet carriage." So we sat in them. It wasn't ideal. I understand that people book seats in this car in the hope of peace and quiet. But our hope was that the other passengers would recognize that on a packed train with nowhere else to go, we had two choices: sit here, or place our three-month-old baby in the overhead luggage space.

Even before Charlie made any noise, the woman across from us was harrumphing and tutting and commenting to anyone who would listen that it was supposed to be the quiet car. After about fifteen minutes, Charlie was sweetly burbling away. By which time this woman was losing her shit. Despite the fact that she was wearing earphones playing a tinny version of James Blunt, she could see that Charlie was making some sort of noise and couldn't take it anymore. "Fucking ridiculous," she said to herself and the rest of the carriage. At which point, I felt the need to point out the circumstances of the packed train and that human decency should probably trump her desire to listen to "You're Beautiful" in a sensory vacuum. She disagreed: "Disgusting," she insisted. "Disgusting." I have never felt so uncomfortable. Particularly because the suit across from us looked equally annoyed.

But then something remarkable happened. That same suit turned to the woman and said: "You're the one who's disgusting, where do you want them to go?" Before she could respond, a woman sitting next to her turned to us and said: "It's fine, don't worry, he's not bothering me." And then another woman in the seats behind us: "Me neither, he's a very well behaved little man."

It was as if the woman across the aisle wanted us crucified and the whole carriage stood up to declare: "I'm Spartacus." (Well, maybe not the entire carriage, but at least three people Spartacussed to our aid.)

The tables were turned, and the woman went back to listening to James Blunt, seething.

After a tough couple of months adjusting to our new world, this incident restored something of our faith in people. Me and Lyns talk about it between ourselves, and it has attained mythic status in our minds. It's as if we slayed a dragon. And, in a way, we did. But it wasn't the woman across the aisle who was slayed; it was our fear that we would always be made to feel like we were intruding, always made to feel uncomfortable just because we were in the company of a baby. If we could find that support in the quiet carriage of a train, we could find it anywhere. The people who are dicks about babies are a minority.

So if you are one of the people who stood up to defend a couple of newbie parents on the 16:20 Doncaster to London on December 3 and by some miracle you're reading this, I want to say thank you.

And if you are the stocky woman who was in seat 16A: I want you to know that your taste in music is shit, and that big red blouse you were wearing made you look like a fucking pirate.

GOOD PEOPLE/BAD PEOPLE

In truth, some people just don't like babies. They find them annoying. And I get it. They are annoying. But you know what? There are a thousand things about the outside and my fellow humans that *I* find annoying. (Not least the sound of James Blunt being piped through tinny headphones.) Isn't it true that we have to express tolerance for our fellow man every day? Otherwise, we would all just be wandering around looking to be pissed off at something all the time, and that would make us no better than the people who haunt the comments section of *Breitbart News*.

So, if you are one of those people unable to express tolerance for a mom or dad struggling with their child and you are accidentally reading this book, you should understand something: restaurants, airplanes, buses, shopping centers—these are all public places, they are not your fucking bedroom. We are not hanging out in your house. And if you can't express tolerance for a baby, then you don't have the tolerance to be outdoors. If you're really allergic, then there are a thousand places you can go where you can avoid them: casinos, strip joints, pretty much anywhere after 9 p.m. All the really fun places. Or why not just stay at home so that you don't have to roll your eyes and sigh and make parents feel like shit because their day is not going quite according to plan?

Here is the fundamental truth: no one arrived into the world as a fully formed adult. Not one person. We were all these dribbling, snot-covered, screeching, feral beasties once. And although we can't remember that stage of our lives, I guarantee that every single one of us was disruptive and noisy and really fucking annoying. So, when it comes down to it, to be bent out of shape because you find yourself in the presence of a baby is hypocritical, and you may need to consider the possibility that you're being a dick.

OLD LADIES

At the opposite end of the scale from the eye-rolling baby-haters is a group of people who really like babies. A group of people who can be a great antidote to the negativity of the anti-baby lot: old ladies. Although I joked in the introductory post about avoiding them, to be honest, for the most part it's actually quite pleasant to be stopped by a lovely old lady for a chat and for her to admire your offspring. It's a great way to try out your new role as mommy or daddy and get used to the idea that that's what you now are.

It's also a great way of easing your way back into conversation with adults, since you only need three pieces of information:

1. What is the baby's name?
2. How old is he/she now?
3. What was his/her birth weight?

It's less a conversation and more like they're carrying out a census.

The old lady asking the questions will respond to each answer you give with cooing noises like "awwww" and "ooooh," as if she's recovering from a recent head injury.

In fact, even if you can't remember the answers to these three questions, it doesn't matter—they're not listening anyway. After about the twentieth time of being stopped, I just started making stuff up to see if they were actually paying attention or were just baby-drunk:

"Aaah, what's his name?"

"Wilberforce Fuckleberry."

"Aaah, how old is he?"

"He'll be sixty-two next Michaelmas Day."

"Aaah, how much did he weigh?"

"The same as a large bat."

"Aaaah," they still respond with the glazed eyes and face of a recently satiated paint huffer.

Even though no one's actually listening to me during these conversations, on the whole I enjoy them. These women love Charlie. They really do. They love your baby too. They love all babies, and that's just a really sweet and beautiful thing.

But sometimes you really don't feel like telling the twentieth person that day how much your baby weighed at birth (incidentally, it's always a "good weight"), and other times you just really need to get something done. And on these occasions, lovely old ladies can present a real time hazard. They will happily spend hours just trying to raise a smile from your baby, and generally speaking, let's face it: unlike you, they've got fuck-all else to do.

If you don't want to be rude, avoidance is the best strategy. I mentioned in the introduction that avoiding elderly ladies can be like playing the old arcade classic Frogger (an eighties video game in which you have to dodge hazards to reach your destination). In fact, as the old women in your area get to know you, they begin to be able to spot you from a distance. So around our local streets it has become a lot more like playing Pac-Man.

In our village I now know exactly where the old women live and congregate, and, as there are quite a few of them, I have had to match their cunning and devise a circuitous route to get to and from the shops without being accosted:

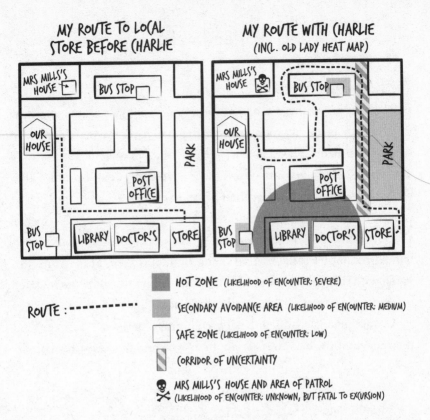

MY ROUTE TO LOCAL
STORE BEFORE CHARLIE

MY ROUTE WITH CHARLIE
(INCL. OLD LADY HEAT MAP)

ROUTE : - - - - - - - - - -

■ HOT ZONE (LIKELIHOOD OF ENCOUNTER: SEVERE)

■ SECONDARY AVOIDANCE AREA (LIKELIHOOD OF ENCOUNTER: MEDIUM)

□ SAFE ZONE (LIKELIHOOD OF ENCOUNTER: LOW)

▨ CORRIDOR OF UNCERTAINTY

☠ MRS MILLS'S HOUSE AND AREA OF PATROL
(LIKELIHOOD OF ENCOUNTER: UNKNOWN, BUT FATAL TO EXCURSION)

This might seem overly complicated, but you underestimate these old women at your peril. The native English old lady is a natural herder, and they tend to hunt in packs. If you don't head for the shops with a solid plan and a route, you can easily find yourself ambushed. Or, much worse, herded into an area heavily populated with other old ladies: hot zones like the post office or the library or, God forbid, the sinkhole of time: the doctor's office, where there's an ever-replenishing army of old ladies. . . . If you get encircled there, you might as well crack open your ration packs and call your partner to request extraction.

So old ladies are a great antidote to the pitchforks and torches of the anti-baby mob, and I think, on the whole, they are more representative of society's attitude toward babies, which is generally positive. Evidence of this positivity can be found in the everyday concessions that society makes to parents, things like drop curbs and parent and baby parking spaces.

CONCESSIONS

The baby-changing room

Baby-changing rooms are one of these concessions. It is amazing how much a baby-changing room sign can mean to parents when their infant has just detonated a level nine in a packed shopping mall. This symbol is a beacon, a light guiding us to a place of refuge. A panic room. Baby-changing rooms can be more than places to change a diaper: they can be rooms to retreat to and regroup. The great ones are pristine, hygienic, comfortable even. These oases of calm have everything on hand, from hands-free antibacterial soap to changing-mat covers. They are illuminated with soft lighting, and calming music plays to soothe the frazzled nerves of the parent. Those are the good ones.

Unfortunately, the good baby-changing rooms are few and far between, and the bad ones are about as welcoming as Death's asshole.

OUTSIDE

You can normally tell, before you even open the door, by its grim handle and the crooked sign above the entrance: ABANDON ALL HOPE, YE WHO ENTER HERE. And, as you open the door, there is a rumble of thunder and a dog howls plaintively in the distance. Welcome to a cubicle of doom.

A flickering strip-light overhead illuminates what appears to be a disused crack house. If you are lucky, there isn't the chalk line of a recent murder victim still visible on the stained floor. You notice one of those "This facility was last checked by" sheets on the wall, but it's just a stone tablet hanging from an ancient cobweb ("This facility was last checked by Pliny the Elder in AD 74").

And, cold, shivering, and wary, you approach the fold-down shelf.

. . . A shelf that appears to have been used by a tramp hosing off his balls. It's fucking filthy. You wouldn't euthanize a dying beaver on this thing, let alone change your baby. (Also, there always seem to be food crumbs in the hinges, like you'd find in an oven door. Who the fuck is feeding their baby on this??)

Who hasn't taken one look into a place like this and opted to change their baby somewhere more appropriate, like the car, or a bench, or a derelict pig-shed?

But sometimes you're desperate. Sometimes there is no choice. So you place the most precious thing in your life onto a surface that has enough bacteria to wipe out France. And demand that your clueless infant not touch anything. As your baby, instead, decides that this is the appropriate time to start pawing everything in sight and licking the walls.

The worst thing about the bad baby-changing rooms isn't even the hygiene level, or the fact that they look like Jeffrey Dahmer's abandoned cellar. It is the fact that nothing is ever replenished. The box of changing-mat covers is empty, the soap dispenser just spits out dust, and you are lucky to find water that's running, let alone hot.

And the design of these places is clearly the job of an idiot. Why is everything out of reach? What is the point of having a big sign saying DON'T LEAVE YOUR BABY ON THIS SURFACE UNATTENDED if you are then going to place the soap, the trash can, the sink, and everything else precisely twelve inches beyond arm's length? The average arm-span of a human is five feet seven inches. Just put everything within that fucking range!!! Jesus.

Even if you and your baby survive the ordeal of changing, there is still the specter of the industrial diaper bin: the throbbing, glowing, radioactive container in the corner of the room, slowly cultivating the virus that fucked everyone over in the film *Outbreak*. Obviously, the foot pedal doesn't work, so you have to use your hands to pry open the lid and close it quickly, before the gas that is released has the same face-melting effect as opening the Ark of the Covenant had on the Gestapo dude in *Raiders of the Lost Ark*.

Baby-changing rooms are supposed to make life easier, and on the whole they do. It reflects well on a society that it wants to soften a new parent's day with this sort of provision. There is no legal obligation to provide these rooms, so clearly businesses believe that they are a good way of encouraging young families with cash to spend to come on in. It seems strange, then, that they go to the trouble of creating such a room and then make it the kind of space that a baddie from *Scooby-Doo* wouldn't take a dump in.

The parking space

Another concession to the struggling parent is the parent and child parking space which can be found outside almost all stores and malls in the UK. They are wider spaces than usual, which means you can get your stroller and baby out of the car without reducing the car parked next to you to scrap, as you repeatedly smash your own car door against it. They are also usefully closer to the entrance if your kids are a bit older and you don't want them wildly running around the parking lot like it's Six Flags. These spaces make sense. At my local mini-supermarket, there are just three parent and baby spaces, placed a few feet from the entrance. And, on the whole, people don't abuse the system. But one persistent offender is always parking his crappy car in one of these slots. Usually the one nearest the door. Almost every other night he's parked in it, so that he can save his legs the thirteen feet extra walking distance to the door. The really infuriating thing is that, judging by his clothes, he's clearly on his way to or from the gym. He's not incapacitated, he doesn't have kids, he's just a dickhead.

On one occasion, I thought about confronting this guy as he went into the shop. But in the end I decided to take the moral high ground . . . on account of him being extremely aggressive-looking and built like a wardrobe. Instead, I did what any right-minded English coward would do and left him a note that I stuck to his windshield:

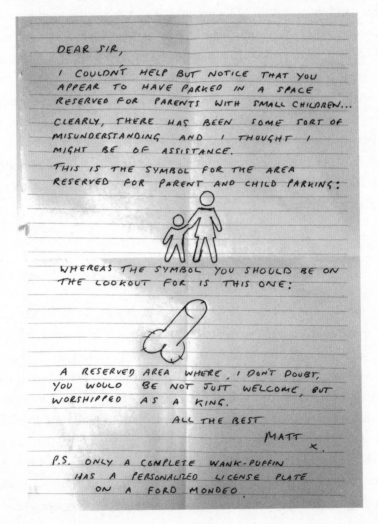

DEAR SIR,

I COULDN'T HELP BUT NOTICE THAT YOU APPEAR TO HAVE PARKED IN A SPACE RESERVED FOR PARENTS WITH SMALL CHILDREN...

CLEARLY, THERE HAS BEEN SOME SORT OF MISUNDERSTANDING AND I THOUGHT I MIGHT BE OF ASSISTANCE.

THIS IS THE SYMBOL FOR THE AREA RESERVED FOR PARENT AND CHILD PARKING:

WHEREAS THE SYMBOL YOU SHOULD BE ON THE LOOKOUT FOR IS THIS ONE:

A RESERVED AREA WHERE, I DON'T DOUBT, YOU WOULD BE NOT JUST WELCOME, BUT WORSHIPPED AS A KING.

ALL THE BEST

MATT x.

P.S. ONLY A COMPLETE WANK-PUFFIN HAS A PERSONALIZED LICENSE PLATE ON A FORD MONDEO.

It's amazing how becoming a parent shifts your perspective and makes you observe your environment and the behavior of others differently. I never really noticed before we had Charlie when someone was parked in a parent and baby space illegally. If I did, I probably thought: *Well, that's a bit unreasonable, I wish that person would show a little more consideration for others.* Now when I see someone without kids parking in one of these spaces, I think: *I hope you die in a Dumpster fire.*

It's a sign of a civilized society that allowances are made for our newest generation; it is an indication of the value that we place on them and their parents. The problem is that this relies on the participation of others: the implicit agreement of the rest of society that there is a decent way of behaving, an understanding that you don't use these spaces if you don't need to.

And, on a serious point, these are the same people who park in disabled spots. Which is a far shittier thing to do than occupying a space for young families. So, if you are one of these people, I ask, on behalf of the rest of civilization, that you take a long hard look in the mirror—and then bash your head against it until you stop being such a massive penis.

EMBRACING THE OUTSIDE

So, for the new parent, the main issue with the outside is the same problem that has always existed with the outside: other people. But not all people, just the usuals: the antisocial, the selfish, the assholes.

Outside is a tricky place, and to begin with it is a place to be feared. And it doesn't help that, in the wild, there are those who will make your excursion harder. Those who will be unhelpful or make you feel inadequate or uncomfortable, as if you are intruding on a space that in truth isn't theirs. But the one thing that all new parents learn quickly is that you have to develop a skin thick enough to deflect the pointy sticks and daggers of other people, and to ignore the minority who would rather you weren't there. Or, better still, embrace all that: the way that people respond to you as a parent, good or bad, helps to make you feel like one.

One thing is certain: you cannot allow inconvenience or the ignorance of others to force you and your baby to stay at home. You invited this incredible creature into the world, so you might as well let that creature see it. And not just for his or her benefit, but for yours. Letting your baby see the wider world can be rejuvenating. Babies watch everything from a sunset to a car wash with wonder. The mundane is transformed into the extraordinary by the way they look at things as brand-new. Hand a baby a blade of grass and watch him turn it over and over in his hand. It's remarkable.

So, for what it's worth, my advice to any new parent? Head out into the world. Experience what it's like to be stopped by lovely old ladies, to be glared at by miserable diners, and to be many, many miles from home with only one wet wipe left and a baby about to enter beast mode.

And when you're ready . . .

Take them farther. . . .

Man vs. Baby, Blog Post: April 20

So, we've just come back from Charlie's first holiday . . . abroad.

One or two people were a bit judgy about the idea of taking a six-month-old away. "So, you're taking him on holiday?" Yeah. "Abroad?" Yeah. "Somewhere hot??" Yeah. "On an airplane???" . . . By which point I was tempted to answer: "No, me and Lyns will be going on the plane, but we thought we'd get Charlie there by driving him to Dover and firing him out of a fucking cannon."

What I actually said was: "It'll be fine." And you know what? It was.

Here's some other stuff I learned holidaying with our tiny human.

We had a checklist for what to pack; it had just one item on it: "Everything."

- Don't take an expensive stroller on a flight. The moment you check in and it disappears behind that rubber curtain, it is collected by two WWF wrestlers who smash it against a wall for half an hour before it is transferred to the runway, where they reverse the plane over it a couple of times before placing it in the hold.

- At your destination, for some bizarre reason you have to collect whatever is left of your stroller (a wheel) from a baggage carousel that's fucking miles away (I'm sure our stroller ended up closer to the airport we'd just left).

- When airlines say they have "baby-changing facilities," what they actually mean is: "a shelf."

- Changing a baby in a plane bathroom is a bit like trying to carve a turkey in a phone box, but half the size of the fucking phone box, having arranged for an incontinent dickhead to bang on the door every five seconds.

- If your baby will sit quietly during the flight, that's great; if your baby will sleep, even better. If, like Charlie, your little one likes to "stand" up all the time, you can look forward to what feels like a midget riverdancing on your bollocks for the next four hours.

- Baby passports are, as I suspected, a rip-off. I've said before that all babies look like Ross Kemp, but the idea that any baby is still going to be recognizable on its passport photo five years after birth is insane. . . . Besides which the immigration people barely even glanced at it. Charlie could have sailed through passport control with a drawing of Gregg Wallace* on the back of a beer mat (and it wouldn't have cost us fifty-odd dollars).

- As for the heat . . . it turns out that taking a baby to a hot country is fine. People in scorching climates have babies quite a lot, so it's a bit daft for us to think that if we take a baby to a sunny place, he will suddenly burst into flames, as if someone's opened the curtains on a vam-

---

*Gregg Wallace is a presenter on *MasterChef UK* and has an oversized, perfectly circular head.

pire. It's just a matter of common sense, shade, avoiding midday, and applying factor thrumpteen sunscreen.

(Just a note on suntan lotion: let it dry off before picking him up or anything; otherwise it's like wrestling a seal that's just left a massage parlor. Charlie was in less danger from the sun than he was from me juggling him like a bar of soap.)

- Even with all precautions, there is a threat from the sun. To you. You will burn. You will be so preoccupied with keeping the sun off the baby . . . You. Will. Burn. As I write this, my face is a haunting red. (I think I applied sunscreen to myself once in the whole week.) In fairness, I did mention to Lyns, before we went, that I wanted to come back with a bit of color. I just didn't particularly want that color to be the same as an angry baboon's penis.

- Sandy beaches are a bad idea. A six-month-old baby puts everything in reaching distance in his mouth, so, in hindsight, sitting him down to play on four acres of powdered glass is a bit dim.

- Unless you're willing to use gaffer tape and a stapler, it is easier to get a squid to wear a fanny pack than to get a baby to wear sunglasses and a hat.

Finally, what I would say to anyone considering taking their baby on holiday is this: Go.

For all its pissy little challenges, to spend time together, away from our newly destroyed home, was incredibly special.

I will always remember Charlie's face as he curled his toes in the sand for the first time. His delight at being pushed around a hotel pool on the back of an inflatable crocodile. And his fascination as we sat on a bench, hand-feeding a sparrow some chips, overlooking the deep blue of the Mediterranean Sea.

Small price to pay that it was the same color blue as my trampled bollocks after the flight home.

7

MAINTENANCE

When I think about what is needed to take care of a baby, I keep thinking about the film Gremlins. *All babies should be presented to their parents in a little wooden box by a wizened old Chinese guy, with some basic instructions: don't get them wet, don't feed them after midnight, and, if you think they've crapped, for God's sake don't pull back the waistband of their diaper to check . . . you'll get shit on your fingers.*

MAINTENANCE

When I was a kid at junior school, there was a tradition that one child would be chosen to take care of the class pet over spring break. I realize now that this was a tradition based on the fact that teachers really don't want to be saddled with a fucking gerbil for two weeks.

Nevertheless, it was considered a great honor to be entrusted with the welfare of the guinea pig, Cracker. Obviously, this job fell to only the most mature, organized, and trustworthy of eight-year-olds. So when I asked Miss Wilson whether I might be considered a candidate, she looked a little bit horrified. What she said was: "We'll see, Matthew, we'll see." When what her eyes were saying was: "Not in a million years, sunshine. You're dressed head to foot in shit from the lost property box, yesterday you swallowed a pencil sharpener, and if I send Cracker home with you, I will be sending him to his certain death."

As the last Friday of the term approached, I was gutted when Emma Mackey was presented with Cracker for the second time that year. I was devastated. Miss Wilson, seeing my disappointment, called me over as I was leaving and said: "Look, Matthew, I've got a very special job for you. I need you to take care of Buddy." She then, with some ceremony, handed over the small potted cactus that had been slowly festering on the windowsill since I'd started at that school three years earlier. . . .

A fucking cactus.

That was how much faith Miss Wilson had in my ability to care for another creature. It wasn't even a regular plant. A fucking cactus. The most indestructible of all plants. Cracker would have needed water, food, daily attention, and affection. Buddy, on the other hand, would survive the onset of a nuclear winter without me even glancing at him (while he cactus-laughed at *me* losing my hair and teeth). But I figured this was my opportunity to demonstrate that I was ready for responsibility. Besides, Miss Wilson had cleverly anthropomorphized the bloody thing by giving it a name. Buddy was my friend.

Needless to say, as I left that day, I didn't want to stuff Buddy into my schoolbag, so I thought I would try to balance him on the handlebars of my bike. Inevitably, as I pedaled away from the playground, Buddy slipped and fell straight under the front wheel of my bike, then he went under the rear wheel of my bike, and, as I reversed to see the damage done, he went back under the rear wheel and then again under the front.

Buddy had been in my care for about fifteen minutes, and now he was lying on the ground looking like spiky guacamole. Buddy was dead.

I think this experience was where my fear of being entrusted with the welfare of a baby came from. Metaphorically speaking, I really didn't want to run over Charlie on my bike.

THE SMALL STUFF

I knew that the maintenance of a baby would not be simple. That it would take organization, conscientiousness, and common sense. All things which, as a child, I was lacking, and as an adult I am still working on.

MAINTENANCE

As it turns out, babies are surprisingly robust. But the upkeep required to keep them alive does make looking after a cactus, or a guinea pig for that matter, look like child's play. With babies, you can't just water them. Or pop them in a cage, put down some straw, and exercise them by putting them in a massive wheel. It's more complicated than that.

All parenting books give you advice about the big stuff: how to feed a baby, how to change her diaper, how to get her to sleep. But most of them don't talk much about the small stuff that's required day to day: how to dress him, how to bathe him, and in general how to stop him from looking like a miniature hobo. All that is stuff you learn on the job.

And it's not straightforward stuff. Babies don't want to be clean, they don't want to be dressed, they don't want to have their nails clipped or their noses wiped. All of this stuff annoys the shit out of them (and nothing is potentially more explosive than a six-month-old being mildly inconvenienced). So the simplest of things becomes a daily battle and maintenance an ongoing war. But, as in every battle, strategy is everything.

The great Chinese military strategist Sun-tzu once wrote, in *The Art of War*, that to win any conflict, "You must swoop like a Falcon . . . move swift as the Wind, attack like the Fire and be still as the Mountain."

It is thought that, in these words, Sun-tzu was describing how he achieved a great victory over the Chu army in the Battle of Boju in 506 BC. But, according to historical record, Sun was a parent, so he may well have been describing a strategy for dealing with a baby that doesn't want its nose wiped or its face cleaned. Faced with this ultimate foe? If you don't swoop like a falcon, you don't stand a chance.

BATHTIME

According to our old friend the Baby Whisperer, babies "don't really get very dirty."

I beg to differ. Maybe Charlie is an exception but, from what I've seen, when babies reach the age at which they are eating solids, they tend to finish most days in a kind of cracking cocoon of crap. A mix of liquids, bodily accretions, and food congeals around their body which, as it dries, leaves them barely able to move at the joints.

With this in mind, there is a fierce debate online among parents as to how often it's necessary to bathe a baby. It's a debate largely sparked by a mom blogger in the US who wrote that she only bathed her newborn once a week, if that. Which I just can't imagine. Again, I'm in no position to judge anybody for their parenting decisions, but I can only imagine that after a week without a bath, her kid must look like some sort of feral, mat-haired spider monkey, which, if it escaped, would spook the neighbors into calling pest control to catch it in a big net. But this woman and her many supporters are adamant that, when it comes to bathing your baby, once a week is enough. (And they are probably just annoyed that you can't take your tot out into the back garden and hose him down, without Child Protection Services sticking their nose in.)

The official advice, in the UK at least, is to bathe your baby a minimum of three times a week. But for a lot of us, bathtime is the daily touchstone of the evening routine. As much a vital part of that routine as alcohol consumption and pretending to be deaf when your partner says that it's your turn to tackle the diaper bin.

Baby bathtime has always conjured images of splishy-splashy fun: grinning wet babies wearing foam beards and hats and expressions of delight. And it's true that it can be a really enjoyable task for both parents and baby. It is also one of those rare daily responsibilities that experts are right in saying can be a great time for bonding.

But sometimes, after a long day following expert advice to bond over diaper-changing, playing, dressing, reading, tummy time, and feeding, there comes a point where even the most patient of parents must think: *Okay, can everyone stop bloody bonding for a minute and let's get the yogurt and SpaghettiOs out of this kid's chin folds?* Not every moment is a moment.

Particularly as the window of opportunity for splishy-splashy fun is quite a small one. The joy of bathtime doesn't really begin until babies can sit up on their own. Before that, they just lie there, splayed on their backs and looking confused. At this early stage, a baby doesn't appear to be having much fun at all and looks more like a frog that has regained consciousness mid-dissection.

So, maybe newborn bathtime is just not as much fun as it's made out to be. But it is straightforward. The hardest thing you have to do is support her head, or put her in a little waterproof seat thing that sits in the water.

But then one day your baby can sit up on his own, and he is suddenly alert to the fun of his echoey surroundings. He gently splashes and plays with the confused menagerie of ducks, sharks, and squirty dolphins (and other plasticky bath crap that outnumbers him ten to one). And this is the window of opportunity in which to get those treasured snaps of a happy baby, cheerfully playing as he sits in the tub.

Because, before long, he can stand up as well and is no longer content to sit still in the water. He doesn't want you to hold him, and he certainly doesn't want to be washed. And, by the way, you can stick your little waterproof seat thing up your ass.

HOW TO BATHE YOUR BABY

Fortunately, we covered "How to bathe your baby" in our parenting classes. I remember it mainly because our tutor, Barbara, announced that she had an "acronym" that spelled out the things to remember. She then wrote "T.D.C.T." on the whiteboard. Which isn't an acronym at all, because acronyms are supposed to be pronounceable (like NATO or NASA). I know this is pedantic, but what actually annoyed me was that she then revealed that the initials stood for "**T**emperature, **D**epth, **C**leaning, and **T**owel." And it occurred to me that instead she could have said "**T**emperature, **W**ater Depth, **A**blutions, and **T**owel." Which would actually *be* an acronym. And it would also have spelled out how I felt as a forty-year-old man in a classroom on a Saturday morning, being taught how to use a towel.

Temperature

Making sure that the temperature of your baby's bath is correct is obvious, but really important. A baby's skin is incredibly sensitive to heat and cold. So, as Barbara pointed out, you can't run a bath at the same temperature you would enjoy yourself; it's just way too hot for them.

Speaking personally, I just don't enjoy a soak unless it takes several layers of skin off as I get in. In fact, it's amazing we were ever able to conceive at all, given the temperature I like my bath to be. Doctors say that when attempting to conceive, it's important to keep your testicles at a cool temperature. But, over the years, I've enjoyed regular baths that have been so hot I may as well have been tea-bagging Mount Vesuvius.

(Lyns is the same. I don't mean she's been dropping her balls in a volcano, I just mean we both like a bath that is about the same temperature as the earth's core.)

Obviously, these sorts of temperatures are no good for a baby. You're trying to clean them, not make a soup. So you have to be really careful.

The recommended temperature is 98.6 degrees. Which, according to Barbara, can only be accurately measured using your elbow. For some reason, the elbow is the "go-to" joint when you need to accurately measure temperature.

I know that parents have relied on the miraculous temperature-gauging powers of the elbow for centuries, but I'm not convinced. It's not as though the elbow is some hypersensitive erogenous zone. In fact, it strikes me as a particularly unsensitive area of the body to be taking such an important measurement.

Besides, you can buy bath thermometers for next to nothing, and, although Barbara seemed a bit suspicious of them, my instinct would be to trust the universally constant effect of heat on the element mercury before relying on Barbara's or anybody else's elbow. (After all, when climate scientists want to check the precise temperature of the upper atmosphere or the earth's oceans, they don't toss aside their scientific equipment and say: "Just a second, Bert, we need to be absolutely sure about this. Fuck the calibrated instruments, I'm going in with the middle bit of my arm.")

So while we accepted Barbara's overall point about the importance of the first "T," Temperature, when it came to testing it, we ignored her advice and bought two electronic thermometers: one in the shape of a whale, and one called Beaky (which looks like a bird but I think is supposed to be a platypus).

And, despite the unwavering accuracy of Beaky, and the unquestioned reliability of Willy the Whale, I still make sure to confirm the temperature of Charlie's bath with my bloody elbow before he gets in. As the Barbara in my head says, "You can't be too careful."

Water depth

The depth of the water should be "deep enough to cover the baby's waist while sitting." The recommendation is about five inches. (An easy way to remember is that it's roughly the same depth as fans of *Real Housewives*.)

When I was a kid, I used to be bathed in the kitchen sink. I don't know whether this is a northern thing, but I think it was once quite common. And, when I think about it now, it makes perfect sense. The kitchen sink is the ideal baby bath. It is the perfect depth. Not just that, but it's also well contained—there isn't really anywhere for a baby to go—and, vitally, it's also at an ideal height (so, unlike constantly leaning into a bathtub, it doesn't make your back feel it's about to snap like a stressed Wasa crisp). In almost every way the kitchen sink is a lot safer and much more convenient than using a full-size bath.

All that said, despite its many advantages, we don't bathe Charlie in the kitchen sink. I suggested it to Lyns, but she informed me that this wasn't the 1930s, and I should stop being nostalgic about my happy days sharing a bath with cutlery and pans.

Lyns was insistent that, instead, we follow Barbara's suggestion to use a plastic baby bath. Which, in fairness, performs similarly to the sink. Basically, you put it in the main bathtub and then put the baby in that. It doesn't solve the problem of crippling back spasms, but it does mean you can bathe a baby at the requisite five inches without filling a full bath, and also keep him reasonably confined and manageable. It's no kitchen sink, but it makes sense.

We bought ours online for twenty dollars. It's called something like the BubbleTime EazeeBath. It's basically a bucket. A twenty-dollar bucket, but still a bucket. And if you think that for twenty bucks it's got to be more complicated than that—it's not. Here are the comprehensive instructions that it came with: I'm not kidding, a single page that consisted of these two diagrams:

Which as far as I can make out mean:

1. "Fill it with water."
2. "Don't put your baby in it and fuck off to a seventies night."

MAINTENANCE

Ablutions/cleaning

One of the main pieces of childbirth advice about cleaning your baby is that with a newborn, you should clean with particular attention to the charmingly named "umbilical stump" (the nub of the cord that is left behind on a baby's belly button).

I'll be honest, at the time of attending childbirth classes I didn't really know what an umbilical stump was, so I didn't question the handy hint and tip that followed (if I had known, I might have raised a hand).

But, according to Barbara, the umbilical stump often drops off while being cleaned and, when it does, some parents like to keep it as a souvenir.

Really? A souvenir?

I understand keeping a lock of hair, or even a first tooth, but I've never seen one of those beautiful, shabby-chic keepsake boxes with lovely, scrolly writing on the front that reads: UMBILICAL STUMP. Sorry if you've got one of these things in a shoebox or a jar of formaldehyde in the cellar, but unless you happen to be an avid collector of scabs and other necrotizing dead flesh, I'd trash it. It's weird.

The only other piece of significant parenting advice with regard to bathing our baby was this: "Clean thoroughly"—advice that I thought lacked the necessary detail to tackle a soap-coated baby who is pretty adamant about *not* being "cleaned thoroughly." A task that, you would have thought Barbara might have mentioned, can be like wrestling a pissed-off alligator that's been coated in butter.

So even if you've got your baby in an overpriced bucket, filled to a depth of a perfect five inches and at a temperature of a balmy 98.6 degrees, the cleaning bit is easier said than done.

Charlie likes to splash. A lot. Consequently, one of the drawbacks of bathing him is that whoever is responsible often ends up drenched. When he was tiny, so long as you remembered to roll up your sleeves, the chances were you could avoid getting wet at all. (Maybe you would get a little damp at the edges of your rolled-up cuffs as you gently cradled his head.) But then Charlie reached the age where being in the bath became something exciting and splashtastic, and since that point there has often been no way to avoid getting soaked. Rolling up your sleeves is an exercise in futility (it's like walking into a collapsing building and pausing for a moment to put a bobble hat on). Now, if the mood takes Charlie, whoever's turn it is to bathe him walks out of the room looking like they've just been at sea in a storm and had to tether themselves to the ship's wheel to prevent getting tossed overboard.

But that's nothing. The moment you try to get him clean or produce a washcloth, he unleashes a tempest and thrashes around like someone has just dropped an electrical appliance into the bath or he's being pulled under by Jaws.

It's even worse when he's tired. If you fancy a challenge, try getting some lovely stock photos of foamy-splishy-splashy time when you're handling a soap-covered baby who is overtired and furious that play has been interrupted for cleaning time. (We've got a couple of snaps, but they're blurred by water spray and out of focus and it's hard to make out whether we're bathing a baby or fighting off a kraken.)

Actually, maybe the woman who bathes her spider monkey once a week is onto something. . . .

Towel

Finally, the last segment of the lesson, the final "T": Towel. There wasn't much to this bit of the lesson either. It consisted of: dry your infant thoroughly, keep him warm. Oh, and use a hooded towel. Because, for some reason, after every bath you have to dress your baby as Emperor Palpatine.

So, that's roughly how to bathe a baby and keep him clean. But it's not the only way you can keep your offspring from looking like a twelfth-century cave dweller.

FINGERNAILS

After bathtime is a good time to tackle fingernails. When we first left the hospital, we were given a little starter kit by friends who had recently had a baby of their own. It had all the essentials: a first baby romper, a first bib, a little hat and bootees—and also a full miniature nail kit with nail clippers and a file. I thought it a bit odd at the time, a manicure kit for a baby. I mean, how often could you possibly need to trim a baby's fingernails? Answer: constantly.

You know how fast Wolverine deploys his claws? That's basically the same speed that a baby's fingernails grow. You can cut them, file them, angle-grind them: turn your back for five minutes, turn back again, and there your little one is—a mini Edward Scissorhands, lying in his crib and raking his own face until he looks like one of the Cenobites from *Hellraiser*.

And this is the problem: the speed at which newborn babies' nails grow wouldn't be such a great issue if clawing at themselves wasn't their favorite hobby.

In the first few months of Charlie's life, I'm sure our health visitor was beginning to think that, in between her visits, we were entering him into underground knife fights. Every time she asked how things were going and we replied that everything was fine, I kept waiting for her follow-up question to be: "Really? So, how come he looks like you've locked him in a cupboard with a fucking puma?"

What she did say was that, in fact, it was really common. Babies like to scratch themselves—they just do. And she suggested a few solutions. We tried "scratch mitts," but there was more chance of keeping a pair of sunglasses on Voldemort. And we tried rolling his sleeves over his hands, but he really hated not being able to put his fingers and thumb to his mouth. In the end, all we could do was try to keep his nails under control: trimmed, filed, and a little less like the talons of a striking owl.

While trying to find a solution, I saw some pretty bad examples of self-inflicted scratching online; at its worst, it looks like a baby's been wearing the scratchy hat that the Romans made Jesus wear. Also, because a baby's skin is so delicate, even the lightest of scuffs and scratches can look neglectful. But for us, and for most new parents who have this issue, I think the problem is something like the opposite of neglect. To begin with, we failed to cut Charlie's nails adequately, not because we didn't care but because we were worried about hurting him.

His fingers were so small, it felt as though the miniature clippers in our hands were a gleaming machete. The slightest slip, and he could potentially lose a finger or an arm. Trying to clip these teeny-tiny fingernails is like snipping the wires on a bomb. It's stressful and detailed, and the entire time you're waiting for the moment you fuck up, when you snip into baby finger rather than baby nail and blood starts to spray up the walls.

I know that this is all dribblingly crazy—I've never heard of anyone who has hacked off one of their kiddy's fingers while giving them a manicure. But when you're a new, inexperienced, and clueless parent, sharp stuff near your baby is alarming and viscerally unwelcome and any danger is exaggerated tenfold. It's the same reason we haven't given our little boy his first haircut, because that would mean bringing him within three feet of scissors. (And that's despite the fact that he has a blond nest at the front and a rampant mullet at the back. He looks like a redneck Boris Johnson. . . . Now, that's neglect.)

Over the last few months, I've actually got quite good at clipping Charlie's nails. Maybe because he's older, it's a bit easier, simply because his fingers and fingernails are bigger. And maybe practice just makes perfect. Whatever the case, I've not hurt him yet, so it's probably true to say that fear of doing so was just a new parent's dim paranoia.

Just a word on toenails: they are almost as bad. In fact, in some ways they're worse because you don't notice them as frequently. Also, they seem to grow in spurts, so they can get quite long before you suddenly realize you've been ignoring them. We didn't cut Charlie's for a while, and they ended up a bit longer than you would probably want. But I think other parents must make the same mistake. Because a few weeks ago I took him to a soft-play area in our village, and noticed that the kids without socks on had similarly long toenails. One kid was making a skittering sound, like a dog that hadn't been walked in years. Charlie's weren't good, but you could have hung this kid from the rafters like a bat.

COLDS, COUGHS, AND SNIFFLES

It seems a really obvious thing to say, but the worst thing about a baby being unwell is the simple fact that it makes him unhappy. And when babies first become ill, it is one of those times that you really notice that as parents your happiness is now contingent upon *their* happiness. That you would now give anything to take the misery that they are feeling and wear it for them. To make matters worse, babies are unable to tell you how they feel, what hurts most and where. And you in turn are unable to comfort them in the most important of ways: which is to let them know that the way they feel is temporary and it will all be okay again soon.

But one thing all new parents have to get used to is dealing with the colds, coughs, sniffles, and low-level illnesses that afflict a creature who has a secondhand immune system. I say secondhand, because most of a baby's immunity comes from its mom. A baby's own immune system is about as effective as a missile defense shield made of Pringles. It's why kids always seem to have a perma-cold, always seem to be watery-eyed and blowing snot bubbles the size of an astronaut's helmet.

A kid with a cold is pretty disgusting. The hagfish defends itself against predators by producing its own body weight in slime, and once a baby's nose starts streaming the Day-Glo gunk of a cold (to add to all the other fluids they produce), it's much more like dealing with a threatened hagfish than a human.

And when a baby is not blowing snot bubbles, or creating gluey strands of the stuff that stretch like pizza cheese between your shoulder and his face, he is cultivating solid boogers so big it is almost as though the baby has been built around them, rather than the other way round.

One thing that came as a surprise to me was the fact that babies can't blow their own noses. I don't mean excusing themselves and drawing a handkerchief from a breast pocket, I mean snorting outward. They can't do it.

So it becomes your job to dislodge and remove the stuff that is causing any blockage in their nasal passages. One more disgusting job to add to all the other disgusting jobs that are now your responsibility (responsibilities that if you were told they would be yours in a job interview, you would punch the interviewer in the face).

Amazingly, there are tools to help you perform this task. There are various types. There is one that you hook up to a vacuum cleaner. Another that consists of a clear plastic tube that you stick up your baby's nose and then suck on the other end, siphoning snot from your baby like you're stealing gas from a parked car. There are others, but we use one called a "nasal aspirator." It's quite difficult to describe what it is, but it's basically a rubber bulb with a plastic tip on the end. You squeeze the bulb and then stick it up the baby's nose, and as you release your grip it's supposed to use suction (like a plunger) to draw the blockage out.

(Again, maybe it's a new parent's paranoia, but to begin with I was worried that if I allowed the thing to suck too hard, or put it too far up his nose, I might create some perfect vacuum and suck out Charlie's brains.)

Once you get the hang of it, it's a bit like fishing. And it's horribly satisfying when you snag a monster. I once latched onto something that felt like it was a carrot stick or piece of Lego, only to discover the largest booger ever created. This thing was roughly the same size as the asteroid that Bruce Willis landed on in *Armageddon*. And it fought. It fought hard. This was Moby Dick to my Captain Ahab. And when I landed it, I even saved it to show Lyns. But she just patted me on the shoulder, told me to go and have a pint and get out of the house for a while.*

The cold virus is one of nature's greatest success stories, designed to spread itself with incredible efficiency. And there is no greater agent of spread than a baby, who coughs and splutters like a germy lawn sprinkler, without regard for who is in the vicinity. Babies don't cover their noses when they sneeze or put their hands to their mouths when they are cough-hacking away like a two-pack-a-day truck driver. This is how the perma-cold is passed around the household like in a game of tag. Because, with a lack of sleep and poor diet, there is no defense for the parent either, and misery descends on all. Not least because it fucks up the progress you were making with "the routine."

---

*In England, all major personal crises are solved by going to the pub and having a pint; it is our alternative to therapy. (Apparently, in the US there is approximately one bar for every 5,000 people. In the UK it's more like one pub for every 300 people. We have more pubs than grocery stores. Come the end of the world, we'll all starve to death . . . but will probably be too drunk to give a shit.)

Apart from general misery, this is the main problem with coughs and colds: the interruption to a routine you were slowly creating the way you were told to. Feeding your infant and putting her to bed at a certain time goes out the bedroom window. Just when she was starting to show signs of "sleeping through," she is now stirring as frequently as she ever did. Even if she does sleep an Infants' Tylenol–induced few hours, your own sleep quota is once more back to those first few weeks, when you could not close your eyes for worry. We are returned to those terrifying early days when the baby stops audibly breathing for what seems to be hours. When a breath in is followed by a breath out, but not necessarily in that order and with stretched time between the two. Even if you are able to sleep through the worry, it's unlikely you can sleep through the noise, as you are now sharing a sleeping area with a coughing, wheezing baby with a blocked nose that sounds like an accordion getting dry-humped.

As far as the low-level illnesses that afflict a baby go, it's not just the colds, sniffles, and coughs that parents have to deal with. There are the fevers, the cradle cap, the diaper rash that looks like radiation burn, the side effects of teething, and all the other miscellaneous spots and rashes that are all meningitis until Googled not to be. All these unwelcome symptoms provide a source of anxiety and concern that add to a new parent's gray hair and bubbling blood pressure. But, thankfully, there is a means of defense against some of the more serious stuff.

IMMUNIZATIONS

This is tough.

Just when you have built up a modicum of trust between you and your offspring, you have to destroy it all by holding them still while a stranger jabs them in the leg with a sharp stick.

I was responsible for taking Charlie to get his vaccinations (Lyns is terrified of needles and has been known to pass out at the sight of someone sewing). As a parent, I found it to be one of the hardest things I've had to do so far. As Charlie felt the nip of the injection, his bottom lip trembled, and as he geared up to scream he delayed for a moment. Just long enough to look me in the eye with the disappointment of a thing betrayed. *Et tu, Brute?*

I completely understand why parents are put off going through this ordeal. But it's not really an ordeal, apart from the rare instances of allergy and reactions. For the most part, babies cry for a bit, and then they see a bug on the wall or a leaf and forget the whole thing. Or maybe, as in Charlie's case, they have a fever and feel under the weather for a day or two. But, on the whole, the only damage done is to the parents, who convince themselves that they have performed some sort of treachery.

Unfortunately, what puts some parents off having the vaccinations isn't the guilt at causing a moment of pain or a couple of days of fever. It is more likely to be the link between immunizations and the onset of autism or other serious disorders. And, as far as this is concerned, I would say it's best not to worry about it. Because there isn't a link. At all. Not one.

What there is, is some discredited, shitty research that has proven to be fraudulent. And a vast amount of excellent research showing that, in fact, there is no more a scientific link between vaccinations and autism than there is between eating Cinnabons and going cross-eyed. No link. At all.

Now, you may be reading this thinking: *What do you know? The one thing we've established reading this book is that you're something of an idiot.* And that's true. But the overwhelming majority of scientists and doctors contend that vaccinations save lives and are not dangerous. As Jimmy Kimmel once said, when it comes to vaccinations: "If you really believe that 99 percent of doctors are dishonest, you need to see a doctor."

But choosing to vaccinate their child is a decision that every parent must make. And, in fairness, there are still some proponents of the opposing view, people who argue that vaccinations are fundamentally dangerous. These people are called "anti-vaxxers."

So, in the interests of balance, these are some of the esteemed researchers and proponents on each side of this controversial debate.

On one side, proposing that vaccinations are overwhelmingly safe, are:

- The World Health Organization
- The United Nations
- The Centers for Disease Control (US)
- The National Health Service (UK)
- The General Medical Council (UK)
- The British Medical Association
- The American Medical Association
- The American Academy of Pediatrics

On the other side of the debate are:

- A man who thought he was the son of God, but now believes that the Royal Family are Lizard People: David Icke
- Boko Haram
- Star of *Scary Movie 3*: Jenny McCarthy
- The Taliban
- And, finally, a man famous for being a racist, backward man-child and having hair like someone has back-combed Bigfoot's asshole: Donald Trump

PERSPECTIVE

When we're dragging ourselves grumpily out of bed at 4 a.m. to deal with a sniffly baby, it can test the patience of all of us. Fortunately, 99.9 percent of the time these illnesses are nothing to worry about and it becomes routine. And immunizations can prevent some of the more serious illnesses—but, unfortunately, not all of them.

So at those moments in the middle of a long night when Charlie is unwell, unsettled, and murdering sleep with greater fury than ever, I try to remind myself of those parents who have to deal with genuine sickness in their children. Parents who would saw themselves in two for a baby that merely woke them at 4 a.m. with a lousy bloody cold, rather than with a genuine illness that can't be nose-wiped away. I try to remind myself how incredibly fortunate we are that Charlie is healthy and well.

I *try* to remind myself of those poor, desperate parents. But usually I don't succeed. And if I'm woken up at 4 a.m. tomorrow night by a snuffly baby, I'll probably be complaining under my breath again. Because perspective is a slippery thing. And maybe in this regard, its slipperiness has a purpose. Since to regard our little ones as that fragile is too much of a shitty nightmare to think too hard about.

(For what it's worth, for those of you reading this who have confronted or continue to cope with the nightmare of a genuinely sick baby, I send you my small family's love and admiration, and I promise to try harder to not be quite such a whiny dick.)

WARDROBE

When Charlie was about four months old, I remember one night trying to dress him for bed. After ten minutes of struggling, I shouted to Lyns for help. And as she peered around the nursery door, I complained that the new sleepsuit/grow-bag things she'd bought were faulty and would probably need to be returned. It took Lyns about a second to work out that the item of clothing wasn't faulty at all, and a further second to realize that I'd spent the previous ten minutes trying to dress Charlie in a pillowcase. "You're a moron," she patiently explained. Charlie raised one eyebrow in agreement.

The disappointing thing about this episode was that, at this point, I thought I had started to "get it."

I'd begun to understand things like turn-over scratch sleeves and "envelope necks" (this is a design of onesie that means you can remove it by pulling it downward, rather than over the baby's head—so if there's shit on the onesie, you can take it off without coating his face in it). But the pillowcase incident was a reminder to not get too cocky, that there is always something new to learn. And if you don't keep up, one day your kid will end up sitting in his baby sensory class wearing bedding.

A lot of threads

The sheer volume of clothing a baby can get through is a shock. Before the birth, you buy them more clothes than they could possibly ever wear. And then they get through them in no time at all. This is partly because, as we've already covered in graphic and nightmarish depth, babies expel fluids at a fairly constant rate, so they need changing a lot. But it's also because they grow exponentially. Older parents say it all the time: that their kids grew in the blink of a wistful eye. That one minute their little one was crawling, the next he was six feet tall and being brought home by police after being caught smoking weed on the hood of his friend Dean's car. (Sorry, Mom.)

But they never grow faster than in those first few months. Babies grow at an insane rate during this time, outpacing the speed at which you can wash or buy clothes. In the first six months, they double in weight, and by the time they're one year old they are one and a half times taller than when they first arrived. To put that in perspective: if they continued to grow at that same rate as they got older, by the time they were ten years old they would be twenty-two yards tall. Which is about the same height as the BFG or a small apartment building. (Try buying clothes for your child then. Even Big and Tall doesn't cater to that level of freakery.)

So imagine how many clothes *you* would need if you doubled your waist size every six months and doubled in height every couple of years. Oh, by the way, as if you could forget, you shit yourself three times a day. It's a lot of duds.

Given how many clothes they get through, and how expensive it can be to keep up, when shopping for an item of baby clothing, a parent's priorities must always be the same: How much is it? Is it machine-washable? How long will it last? How easy and quick is it to get on and off?

And, once you're aware of those priorities, you do what everyone else does: ignore them and buy expensive, impractical shit that your baby looks cute in.

Fashion

When it comes to items of baby clothing, practicality is always secondary to whether or not a baby will look cute in it. And the fashion industry has either caught on to or driven this demand. Of course, babies are too young to have a preference for any particular fashion themselves, so we imprint our own style onto them. With Charlie, you can tell at a glance who has dressed him that morning. If Lyns has dressed him, he will look preppy and smart; if I've dressed him, he will be dressed as Batman.

But this tendency we have to imprint our own tastes and interests onto our children's wardrobes leads to criticism. Just recently, I read an article about how new parents are supposedly treating their children as "vanity projects." The writer argued that, by choosing clothes according to our tastes and interests, we are treating our children as no more than accessories to be embellished to gratify our own egos. First, I think that's quite a miserable view to take, and second, I just don't think it's true. When we dress a baby according to our own tastes or buy them a Spider-Man outfit, a football jersey, or a sloganed T-shirt that reflects our sense of humor, I don't think we're accessorizing them. In fact, I think we're defining our son or daughter as an important member of our tribe, and I think that's a positive thing, rather than something to be discouraged and made to feel like a dick about.

But maybe we also dress our children in things we can't get away with wearing ourselves. Stuff that as adults we would like to wear, if only the world weren't such a judgmental, boring, and piss-on-your-chips kind of place.* Thanks to my lifelong obsession with comic books, Charlie is often dressed in superhero garb or as a storm trooper, but maybe it's only the rules of social conformity that stop me from going into work each day dressed the same.

Also, I suspect that when some women (and maybe some men) are purchasing a princess- or ballerina-inspired outfit for their three-month-old little girl, there is a small part of them that is wishing that they lived in a world in which they could wear something just as magical (without being committed). Even if this "vanity project" theory is true, I still think it's really unfair to say that we're treating babies as accessories. By dressing them in these cheery, wondrous ways, it is much more like we are dressing them without constraint. With simple fun.

But, as in all things, there are those people who have all the common sense of a doorknob. People who miss the point and take things

---

*The uniquely British expression "piss on your chips" comes from the scenario of a guy buying some takeout chips (French fries) after an evening's drinking. Finding that he needs to pee on his walk home from the pub, he places his chips on the ground and then accidentally urinates on them. Hence, "piss on your chips." What can I say, English is a beautiful language.

too far, and who should be discouraged from dressing themselves, let alone their innocent infants.

100% Bitch

I was in the waiting room of a doctor's office a while ago and noticed a little girl about the same age as Charlie, sitting in her stroller wearing a onesie with a slogan emblazoned on the front that read: "My mom's the Queen Bitch, and I'm her princess."

Okay, far be it from me to question the clothing choices of royalty. But it strikes me as one thing to express your own personality through the clothing your kid wears, and quite another when you have a personality that celebrates being ignorant.

The definition of *bitch* is:

[bich] noun: a lewd, immoral, malicious, spiteful, or overbearing woman—sometimes used as a generalized term of abuse

Reading that definition, I find it utterly baffling that you would celebrate this as a character trait, let alone proudly display that trait across your innocent child. (I looked up to see what kind of parents would do something like that. I wasn't that surprised to discover an aggressive-looking woman eating a grab-bag of Tostitos. And a guy, presumably the dad, looking on gormlessly, as though you would need to put his two brain cells in the hadron collider and smash them together for him to stand a chance of a coherent thought. *Aaah,* I thought, *that explains it: they're idiots.*)

The most surprising thing was that this was not a custom-made T-shirt. It's available to buy online right now, and you can buy all kinds of baby-wear that expresses similar sentiments: baby rompers with slogans that read: "100% Bitch," or "If you think I'm a bitch you should meet my mom," and so on. If you've ever dressed your baby in one of these things, this may well come as a surprise to you, but when most normal-thinking people see a baby wearing a onesie that reads "100% Bitch," they don't actually think that the baby is a 100 percent bitch . . . but they do think that the parents of that baby are 100 percent dumb as fuck.

In looking up this weird subfashion of bitchwear, I discovered that when it comes to inappropriate clothing for babies, a baby romper that displays the slogan "100% Bitch" is actually pretty tame.

Quiz question: Which of these baby onesies are available for sale online right now?

Answer: All of them.

So, if you're reading this and you're still confused as to what is and isn't appropriate clothing to dress your new arrival in, here's a useful rule of thumb:

> *Appropriate:* Pastel clothing with cartoon characters and fun slogans that express how much your child is loved and cared for.
> *Inappropriate:* Clothing with slogans that reference wrecked vaginas and mommy's reluctance to perform oral.

Stick with that, and you will probably not go too far wrong.

So fashion for babies is a real thing, a multibillion-dollar industry that caters to all walks of life. And, within reason, you might as well express your own style through your baby's wardrobe, because by the time they are toddlers they won't be seen dead in the stuff that you choose anyway. In the modern world, apparently, kids as young as two have an input into what they want to wear and have developed their own style by the time they reach pre-K. It's the way things are.

Which is not fair.

I don't mean to digress, but when I was a youngster, from the moment I was born, I was almost permanently dressed like a dickhead. My mom and dad didn't seem to give anything like the thought that is now given to clothing your kids. And it wasn't just when I was a baby that this was an issue. I couldn't have any input into my own clothes until I was a teenager, and before that point my parents used to dress me as if it were a punishment.

Here's a picture of me aged nine. I'm wearing: a burgundy crushed-velour V-neck sweater with elbow patches, a wide-necked white shirt that looks like a fucking albatross has landed on my neck, and tartan flannel shorts.

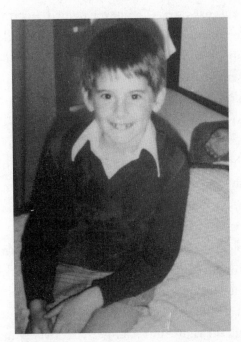

Out of shot is what I was wearing on my feet, which was always knee-high gray socks and brown sandals.

I can't think of any reason for dressing me like this other than to ensure that I was bullied. I would often enter the school gates to shouts of: "Coyne, you look like a fucking dweeb!" And that was just from the head of the math department, Mr. Glover.

When it comes to his wardrobe, Charlie doesn't know he's born.

Practicality

As I mentioned earlier, the main problem with modern baby clothes is that cuteness is very much the priority, and practicality is so often an afterthought.

It's why idiots like me and Lyns buy a baby a pair of denim overalls. Only a moron, or someone with no experience, buys a baby the impractical horror that is a pair of denim fucking overalls. These things are less an item of clothing and more something that Houdini would have attempted to escape from, as he was lowered upside down into a tank of water. (I've never owned a pair, but I bet even adult overall-wearers are soiling themselves on a regular basis, trying in vain to escape from the bastard things when they need the toilet.) We bought them anyway, and then we bought them again. Charlie looked cute in them. Point proven.

If it isn't overalls that are testing your patience, it's the teeny-tiny buttons designed for pixie fingers, or the T-shirts with neck holes that are smaller than a baby's head (so taking them off is like forcing the baby to be birthed again). All of which are minor annoyances by comparison to the ever-present, persistent, tic-inducing and sanity-testing challenge of snaps.

These simple little inventions are a great idea when there are just a couple of them on a onesie, one or two that you quickly pop open to change a diaper. But on some garments, they are everywhere, thousands of the pissy things. All of which need to be lined up correctly, the correct "outy" to the right "inny." Otherwise, twenty minutes into the simple task of buttoning up a onesie, you realize that you got the first one wrong, and now the whole thing's fucked and your baby's arm is attached to his leg, or there's a big gaping hole where his butt is.

Charlie has clothes that take so long to put on that you can start at breakfast and it's getting dark before you've got a leg in. The worst garment we have is an all-in-one romper with a print of a triceratops on the front. This thing is my nemesis. It's very sweet, but it has twenty-four snaps. Twenty-four. I counted them. It's like they are there in place of stitching. Basically, there are no arms, there are no legs, just flaps of material where those things should be and a shitload of these little metal bastards that you are expected to snap together. You essentially have to make the arms and legs yourself as you're dressing him. It's insane. It's one thing to have to button up an outfit while you're dressing your child, but you shouldn't have to manufacture the legs and arms of the clothes at the same time. We might as well set up a loom in the nursery and weave the shit he's going to wear for the day.

I've now hidden this abomination behind the washing machine. But the first time I tried to dress him in the thing, it took an age—an age in which I felt the creeping hand of madness. After ten minutes, I'd developed a twitch in my right eye, and by the time I'd got him half dressed, I was curled up in the corner of the room in a fetal position, quietly weeping. I was wild-eyed, rocking back and forth and gibbering: "They won't line up, Lyns. They won't line up. . . . There's so many of them, you see. . . . They won't line up!!?! . . ." Lyndsay ignored me, snapped the last couple of snaps, and held him aloft: "Ooh, he looks gorgeous."

At what cost, Lyns? At what cost?

The future

There must be a way of making baby clothes more practical and less the sort of grueling challenge that makes you want to drink all day.

Snaps seem to proliferate, but why isn't Velcro used more? As I said in the introduction, if we can make instantly removable, Velcro trousers for male exotic dancers, why can't we do the same for our babies? What kind of civilization are we that we value our strippers over our newest generation?

When I suggested the idea of strippers' clothes for babies on my blog, I got quite a response. (Mainly from people accidentally landing on my page after Internet-searching "male strippers" but still.) People generally thought it was quite a good idea.

But one response in particular caught my eye. It was someone suggesting an alternative idea. (An idea that, on the face of it, sounds like the worst *Shark Tank* idea since Mormon lingerie.) They suggested baby clothes that used magnets.

Ordinarily, I wouldn't reply to someone who sends me a private message extolling the virtues of magnets. I have a siren in my head that goes off when I get messages from crackpots, and enthusiastic fans of magnets are very much in that demographic. But this is actually a real thing. There's a company that makes magnetic clothes for babies. And they work. It's genius. Rather than dick around with snaps, you simply place your baby's arms and legs in the onesie or romper, and they virtually dress themselves as the magnetic buttons come together in that mystical way that magnets do.

Directed by my mystery magnet fan, I saw the video for these clothes online, and my first thought was that they looked impressive. But my second thought was a more excited one: I couldn't help but get quite giddy at the possibility that our baby could be crawling around in his magnetic baby-wear, attracting metal objects to himself (tin cans, cutlery, etc.) as if he had telekinetic superpowers.

So I got in touch with Laura from Magneticbaby and inquired about the possibility that their clothes could turn Charlie into a kind of baby Magneto. I was disappointed.

"[chuckle] Don't worry, the magnets aren't that powerful."

"Well, okay, but . . . well, can you make them more powerful?"

"No. No, we can't."

"Well, why not?"

"Er, for a start, it would probably be quite dangerous."

"Well, how dangerous, becau—"

"I'm hanging up now."

Shit.

So magnetic baby clothes won't give your tot superpowers (for that we still have to rely on good old genetic mutation or a bite from a radioactive spider). But for dressing your kid without becoming a sobbing mental wreck, they may well be the future.

In any case, the good news is that the snap issue seems to be a problem we are well on the way to solving, either through magnetic clothes or through the stripper-inspired Dreamboys line I'm thinking of crowdfunding. And that is a comforting thought. It may come too late for me, and maybe too late for you. But it gives me hope and strength to think that our children's children will never know the indescribable horror of getting to the very last "outy" . . . only to discover that you have completely run out of "innies."

DRESSING

None of the challenges of modern baby clothes would be such a huge issue if, in the process of dressing, your child: Just. Stayed. Still. They don't. Instead, they create the bizarre illusion that they really are all arms and legs and that you're dressing a moody, uncooperative baby Vishnu.

Again, it is fascinating to compare "reality" to "expert advice" and realize that experts ignore the fact that, when the mood takes them, babies can fight being dressed like cornered, syphilitic badgers.

But it's not true to say that babies just flail around to avoid being dressed. In fact, they employ quite sophisticated techniques. Techniques that have the two very specific aims of remaining undressed and making the dresser feel like an incompetent moron.

Returning to *The Art of War*, Sun-tzu once wrote:

Know your enemy and you can fight a hundred battles without disaster.

So studying your own baby's strategies for avoiding being dressed is absolutely vital.

Here are Charlie's current favorite tactics:

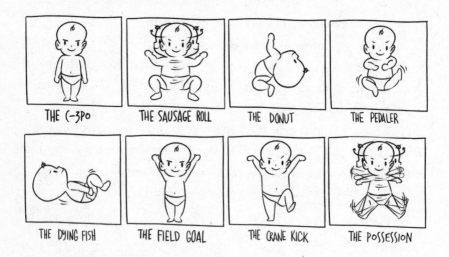

THE C-3PO · THE SAUSAGE ROLL · THE DONUT · THE PEDALER

THE DYING FISH · THE FIELD GOAL · THE CRANE KICK · THE POSSESSION

The C-3PO: Baby stiffens every limb in body and refuses to bend at the elbows and knees. So called because dressing a baby when he deploys this technique is like trying to get a stubborn C-3PO into a wet suit.
Effectiveness: 3/5   *Annoyance Level: 4/5*
Temptation to say "fuck it" and let baby spend the day in just a diaper: 3/5

The Sausage Roll: Baby rolls frantically from side to side, like a stunt-man on fire who's trying to put it out. Simple, but incredibly effective.
Effectiveness: 4/5   *Annoyance Level: 4/5*
Temptation to say "fuck it" and let baby spend the day in just a diaper: 3/5

The Donut: Baby arches back to such a degree that head almost touches ankles and body forms a circle, a human donut, allowing no point of entry for trousers or onesie. (Lacks effectiveness only because the position is a level 10 yogic move and can't be held for very long.)
Effectiveness: 2/5   *Annoyance Level: 3/5*
Temptation to say "fuck it" and let baby spend the day in just a diaper: 2/5

The Pedaler: Baby lies on back and rides invisible bicycle. (Possibly the most infuriating of all the wanky moves a baby can pull if you're trying to put on trousers, socks, or shoes.)

Effectiveness: 4/5   Annoyance Level: 4/5
Temptation to say "fuck it" and let baby spend the day in just a diaper: 3/5

The Dying Fish: A general fucker of a move, as the baby just flips like a trout removed from a pond.

Effectiveness: 4/5   Annoyance Level: 4/5
Temptation to say "fuck it" and let baby spend the day in just a diaper: 3/5

The Field Goal: Baby stubbornly holds both arms in the air, as though awarding a touchdown, and refuses to put them down. (Forcing them down often just forces the energy into the legs and baby simply deploys The Pedaler.)

Effectiveness: 4/5   Annoyance Level: 4/5
Temptation to say "fuck it" and let baby spend the day in just a diaper: 3/5

The Crane Kick: See the 1984 film *The Karate Kid*.

Effectiveness: 3/5   Annoyance Level: 3/5
Temptation to say "fuck it" and let baby spend the day in just a diaper: 3/5

These are Charlie's current favorite moves, but there are many more at his disposal. The Threatened Hedgehog Defense: Curls up into a ball. The Mother Brown: knees up. The Starfish. The Praying Mantis. The Snow Angel. The Condemned Man. You must have a countertactic for each of these.

And then there is a move for which there is no known countertactic:

The Possession: The ultimate. If dressing your child were an arcade game like Tekken or Street Fighter, The Possession would be his "special move." A move in which all techniques are deployed simultaneously. There is nothing any parent can do about this: a demon has seemingly taken up residence in your baby's body and the afore-mentioned demon really doesn't want to wear clothes today.

Effectiveness: 5/5   *Annoyance Level: 5/5*

Temptation to say "fuck it" and let baby spend the day in just a diaper: N/A
(like you have a choice)

Thankfully, Charlie has only resorted to The Possession a few times, but, believe me, they were occasions when he did spend the rest of his day hanging out in just his diaper, with a victorious and smug look on his face.

BABIES HATE CLOTHES

It's difficult to see why babies exhaust so much energy fighting the apparent scourge of being dressed. But the fact is, babies hate clothes. You could argue that that's nonsense, that babies don't hate being clothed, they're just annoyed and irritated by the process of being dressed, but that's not true. Just take a look at accessories.

Every item of clothing that it's possible for babies to remove on their own, they do. Caps, scarves, socks, you name it, babies remove these all the time and at every opportunity. It's as if item by item they are always trying to get naked again. It's what makes baby accessories so absurd. When we take Charlie out, the trail of mittens, hats, shoes, bibs that we leave in our wake is endless. We lose so much of this stuff just on our street that after a walk to the local park, the neighbors see the debris and think they've just missed a streaking dwarf. And you can guarantee that if Charlie could just as easily remove his onesie or pants and toss them aside, he would.

So when you consider the way that babies treat accessories, it is pretty clear that it's not just the activity of being dressed that babies don't like, it is also the actual wearing of clothes that they are not that keen on. So, why?

Maybe the answer lies with those adults who also treat being dressed as an annoyance and being fully clothed as something to be railed against. When you think about nudists, it's hard not to call to mind those occasional documentaries you see about them: the ones with large-breasted lunch-ladies and eighty-year-old geezers enjoying a game of badminton as their old turkey genitals swing in the wind. But maybe there is something to their philosophy that harkens back to this infant state. Perhaps there is something fundamentally unnatural about humans being dressed, and we are all just born nudists, forced to learn to put up with clothes. And maybe this is the battle that is being fought, with such ferocity, between parents and babies on changing mats across the world.

THE MANUAL

If you ever confide in those who have already been through the whole parenting experience, you will often hear the phrase "Yeah, they don't come with a manual." Which begs the question: Why not?

Everything comes with a manual. You can't buy a shitty toaster without a 250-page manual in forty-seven different languages, telling you exactly how to press down the knob on the side, and wait for the bread to turn brown and pop back up.

And yet, when you leave the hospital with this delicate, most complicated and sophisticated of things, you are not given anything that even approaches instructions. You are expected to wing it, to guess, or to seek out the information for yourself in one of the thousands of books that bury practical stuff in talk of psychology and development and bonding.

Maybe that's not a bad thing.

Writers always seem to talk about parenthood as a journey, but I don't think that's quite right. *Journey* implies that you know where you're going or that you have a destination in mind or, at least, that there actually is a destination.

But, when it comes to parenting, it's not at all clear that such a thing exists. We might think that the end point is to steer our children into adulthood; but if you speak to older parents, it's pretty clear that your kids reaching adulthood is just another waypoint, and not a place of arrival at all.

So maybe the traveling is the whole point, and the journey really is just one of discovery. And maybe the fact that you are forced to discover the basics on your own isn't a trick, but a gift. Because when you're on this kind of journey, a manual is the closest thing you can get to a map . . . and traveling with a map? Where's the fun in that?

*   *   *

So, what happened with Buddy?

That day, I rode home in tears. And when I explained to my dad why I was so upset, he made me a cup of tea and told me not to worry.

That weekend he took me to a local garden center, and we bought a new cactus, which we potted in the same glued-together ceramic pot that Buddy had died in. And, after the break, I returned to school and handed a thriving "Buddy Mark 2" to Miss Wilson, who rewarded me with praise, never noticing the switch me and my dad had pulled.

The following semester, on the final day, Miss Wilson called me to the front of the class and presented me with the cage that held Cracker and told me that the class guinea pig was now my responsibility for the whole of the Christmas holidays. I was beyond proud. I felt new, reborn, and I took Cracker home and I lavished him with love and affection and water and food.

And there this story of redemption ends . . .

Or it would have, if I hadn't lavished Cracker with so much attention, love, and food that I seriously overfed him, and six days into the holiday he died of a massive heart attack . . .

HERE LIES
"CRACKER"
TAKEN TOO
SOON

R.I.P.

and so the following day my dad took me along to a pet shop . . . etc.

8

ENTERTAINMENT

"Are you not entertained!?"—Maximus Decimus Meridius

Long before Romans enjoyed gladiators in the Colosseum, human beings have been entertained by the pain and suffering of their fellow man. And I'm starting to think that this is just an instinct we're born with.

I've spent three hours this morning playing with Charlie: pulling faces, tickling him, or playing with one of the thousand toys that are supposed to keep him engaged, and I've barely managed to raise a smile.

But I've just fallen off our garden wall and impaled my ass on an upturned barbecue, and he's been pissing himself laughing for about the last half an hour.

. . . All right, Charlie, stop being a dick now, it really hurts.

ENTERTAINMENT

Peekaboo. Peekaboo. Peeeeekaaahboo. Peeeeeeeeeeeekaaaaaah—you get the general idea.

The peekaboo game is pretty much the ultimate diversion for any discerning baby. It's the pinnacle of entertainment. For a newborn, peekaboo is Elvis's '68 comeback special, it is the Beatles live at Shea Stadium, Bowie at the Hammersmith Odeon in 1973. It is David Copperfield making the Statue of Liberty fuck off before the eyes of the watching world.

There's a good reason why they find this simple game so entertaining: one of the greatest things about babies is that they're quite dim. I know experts stroke their chins earnestly and say babies are extremely intelligent. But, let's face it, the peekaboo game works simply because, when you put your hands in front of your face, a baby generally wonders where the fuck you've gone. Like I said, they're a bit dim. It's not their fault, they've only been on the planet five minutes, so they're still figuring out how it all works. To expect them to do anything other than crap and blow spit bubbles would be like expecting a cat to drive a car: they haven't been taught how, and their feet won't touch the pedals.

So, in terms of entertainment, babies are a great combination: thick, but interested in everything.

Entertaining them is easy then? Nope.

Keeping a baby entertained can be quite difficult. The average newborn has the attention span of a wasted fish. You can make a facial expression that your baby thinks is the greatest, funniest thing she has ever seen. The second time she sees it, it is the dullest, and that can be hard to take. There is nothing more pathetic than an adult trying to gain the approval of a child by blowing raspberries and being ignored. And there is nothing more crushing than being on the receiving end of a withering look from a baby that says: "You're boring me, dick-head."

But it's best not to feel too bad when a baby fails to be impressed by your efforts. Babies can be the toughest crowd ever. If they're not in the mood, it's like doing a stand-up gig for the Taliban:

"Good evening, Kabul! I haven't seen this many beards since Mumford and Sons fucked their way through Amish country. . . ."

Silence, apart from one heckler: "Die, infidel scum!"

So it can be hard work keeping a baby entertained. But there are weapons in our arsenal.

TELEVISION

TV is perfect for babies. It is fast-moving, ever-changing, and characterized by quick edits and high-speed colors. Sit a baby in front of the TV and he is utterly captivated. This box of wonder can turn a hysterical baby into a compliant, calm, and submissive member of the household in seconds. It is the perfect electronic babysitter.

Well, maybe not quite perfect. There is the slight downside that, according to most of the scientific research, too much TV rots babies' brains and leads to them growing up to be gibbering idiots, spree killers, or goths.

Thanks a lot, "Science." Another bonfire you just had to piss on.

In essence, the research suggests that it is all just way too stimulating, and supposedly this can cause all kinds of problems. We might think that our little one is learning about numbers and letters and all that good stuff, but according to these bonfire-pissers, even educational TV can inhibit language development, reading skills, and short-term memory. And, speaking as someone who watched a lot of TV as a kid, I suspect it can also affect your short-term memory. (Ba-dum tish.)

According to HealthyChildren.org, too much television can also contribute to problems with sleep and attention. Basically, if you listen to the professionals, TV is a baby death-ray.

(As conflicting as all other advice seems to be, the experts are in general agreement about this: TV is to baby brains what toffee apples are to teeth. And these same experts make no bones about telling parents that if they let their little ones have unlimited access to telly, it will be their own fault when their offspring grow up to be the kind of goobers who grace the stage of *Jerry Springer*: toothless, in their best sweatpants, and arguing about fuck-all.)

Here's the problem: Charlie loves TV. To begin with he wasn't interested, but then one day he just became transfixed, and if you walked across his line of sight while he was watching *Teletubbies*, he would glare at you like he was considering pulling a blade. This was something of a worry. So, with this development, coupled with the expert advice, we did decide to start limiting the time that Charlie sat in front of the box.

Actually, that's a lie. I'd love to say that we started to limit Charlie's TV intake because of some worthy concern or that it was a decision we reached after a careful study of all the research. But, to be honest, the primary reason we decided to intervene was that we just couldn't take any more of the baffling, nightmarish content of baby television. We could feel our own brains beginning to come undone. Just to be clear, despite the science telling us that TV is a kind of brain-scrambling, domestic lobotomizer for babies, there is such a thing as baby television. Television programming for kids too young to understand the more sophisticated toddler TV of piggy families, trains with faces, and a camp purple dinosaur. (We have all that to look forward to.)

For years I've listened to parents talk effusively about how good kids' TV is, and maybe they were being ironic, or maybe all that later stuff is. But TV aimed at babies is utter dogshit. What babies seem to crave are primary colors, bright lights, and repetition rather than sophistication. Consequently, the whole thing is nonsense. It's all claw-your-eyes-out colors, and trees made of lollipops . . . and this purple thing wanders on and talks like it's had a debilitating stroke . . . and then a unicorn appears and counts to three!? And then there's a badly drawn wizard who shits a rainbow and?! . . . Sweet Jesus!? Just Have A Fucking Storyline!?

Sorry.

But, coupled with sleep deprivation, television for babies is like being strapped to the conditioning chair in *A Clockwork Orange*, and it's easy to see how it can make a baby nuts when, as an adult, watching it even peripherally makes me want to drive a spike through my brain.

All that said, television is not the enemy. As a way of keeping a baby entertained, I can't help thinking it has its place. Charlie still enjoys TV and, while I try to be aware of not turning his brain into mashed potato or the kind of dull organ that sits between the ears of a Kardashian, I see it as a useful tool for a new parent wanting to carve out that short bit of time each day to do something fun like take a piss or eat.

So, to be honest, science can fuck off.

In moderation.

BOOKS

So if TV is no good as entertainment, are books any better?

If you look at the Debate.org website, you will find a lively debate entitled: "Are books better than TV?" It's a good place to start.

It's an interesting intellectual discussion littered with many genuine, what can only be described as "anti-book" comments like this:

"TV is better. Books are long and boring all you do is look at words." Or:

"Books are like just really, really boring like so boring and TV has lots of colors, and it talks to you."

So, there it is, captured in two simple sentences, all the evidence you need that it's really important to read books. Otherwise you'll find yourself about as bright as the people arguing on Debate.org.

Putting the compelling argument aside that books are, like, just really, really boring: in simple terms, when it comes to your baby, science says TV is bad; science says books are good.

And, when it comes to introducing books to your little one, it's a case of the earlier the better.

It is impossible to read a parenting book (or watch a parenting TV show), without being told how important it is to read to your baby from birth as part of your "routine." In fact, some experts go further and suggest you should read to your baby in the womb. The really hard-core parenting professionals suggest you should read to your sperm and unfertilized ovum (not really, I made that up).

I did read to Charlie while he was in the womb, though. We were told it didn't matter what you read because it was all about the baby hearing the cadence and changing tone of your voice. So I whiled away many hours reading to Lyns's belly: *Sandakan: The Harrowing True Story of the Borneo Death Marches*, and also a biography of English gangsters the Krays.

The little one kicked with enthusiasm every time Reggie battered a nonce.* (Again, not really.)

When Charlie was born, we continued to read to him, and still do, every night. And, to be honest, it's not always the most rewarding pastime. For the first few months all a baby wants to do is rip or eat whatever text is placed in front of him. So far, Charlie doesn't give a shit how much room there is on the broom; he cares more about what the pages of *Room on the Broom* taste like. But I am absolutely certain that will change.

My mom read to me as a baby. I don't remember those first books, but then I don't ever remember not being read to as a child. An enjoyment of books is the finest gift she ever gave me (apart from a pair of suede roller skates in about 1989—they were pretty sweet).

I want Charlie to enjoy books as much as I do, and if he does, it will

---

Nonce is British prison slang for a pariah among criminals, usually a sex offender or an informant. It's an acronym for "not on normal communal exercise" and should always be said with a thick cockney accent.

be my gift to him, passed down the generations, to soften the blow of my genetic predisposition to big ears and an intolerance to eggs.

And so I find myself, when it comes to books, finally in agreement with the experts and the scientists. But not for the dry epithets of cognitive development or bonding, but to instill a love.

Ignoring the one you hold in your hand right now, books can be educational and instructive, but at their best they can be redemptive, crushing, life-defining, and perfect. A testament to the best of us, a record of the worst, a eulogy or monument to the very essence of what it means to be human.

Unless it's something by Ann Coulter, in which case it's a load of old shit.

MUSIC

When it comes to entertaining a baby, music may not be treated with the same intellectual respect as books, but it also doesn't suffer from the same stigma or criticism as TV. Depending on the tunes.

These are genuinely Charlie's favorite songs:

"Hotel Yorba"—The White Stripes
"Sound of da Police"—KRS-One
"Homophobic Asshole"—Senseless Things
"Old Time Rock and Roll"—Bob Seger
"Hard to Handle"—The Black Crowes
"Town Called Malice"—The Jam
"Son of Mustang Ford"—Swervedriver
"Suckerpunch"—The Wildhearts
"Ace of Spades"—Motörhead

Fair enough, some of these choices are a bit unorthodox. "Sound of da Police" is a song about racial profiling and police brutality. "Hotel

Yorba" is about a hotel popular with prostitutes and drug users, "Ace of Spades" is about cheating the devil through hard drinking and gambling, and as far as I can work out, "Town Called Malice" is a song about a town in Surrey called Woking.

But these were the songs buried on my iPod that Charlie responded to, and he seemed to enjoy these tunes a lot more than the traditional baby songs about how many monkeys were jumping on a bed, before one fell off and bumped its head. So we compiled this playlist, and we play it while dressing him or changing his diaper (and both me and Lyns often sing and dance around like idiots while we do).

I shared Charlie's playlist on Spotify and mentioned it on the *Man vs. Baby* blog. The response was interesting. A lot of parents shared their own unorthodox song choices, from Johnny Cash to AC/DC to Taylor Swift. But others expressed disgust that we would allow some of these songs to be heard by a baby.

"Sorry, I just don't think it's appropriate [for babies] to listen to. Their brain is a sponge and they pick up on everything."

This was one comment that was typical, and it was an idea that I thought was a bit strange. Charlie may indeed have a baby's loofah-like brain, but it struck me as weird to think that a six-month-old baby listening to the White Stripes is any more or less likely to become interested in drugs. Any more than he is likely to deconstruct the lyrics to "Sound of da Police" and grow to become a toddler that beefs with the local cops.

He just enjoys the beat and the noise of certain songs, that's all. And he responds to the fact that we enjoy them as well.

What strikes me as really odd is that people might be critical of playing a baby these songs but will happily play their own babies traditional nursery rhymes. Traditional tunes that are either crap or, at worst, downright sinister, with regular references to death by choking, decapitation, and encouragements to think that you're a teapot.

Here is a traditional nursery rhyme CD that we bought, imaginatively titled *Traditional Nursery Rhyme CD*. This is the track listing:

TRADITIONAL NURSERY RHYME CD

TRACK LISTING:
BAA BAA BLACK SHEEP
RING A RING O' ROSES
HUMPTY DUMPTY
JACK AND JILL
LITTLE MISS MUFFET
ORANGES AND LEMONS
POP GOES THE WEASEL
HEY DIDDLE DIDDLE
GEORGIE PORGIE
MARY, MARY, QUITE CONTRARY
HICKORY DICKORY DOCK

So, keeping in mind the criticisms of playing modern music to your baby, I looked up the meanings of some of these catchy numbers:

"Ring a Ring o' Roses" (a.k.a. "Ring Around the Rosie"): This is a cheery little tune about the spread of the bubonic plague. The lyrics are basically a list of symptoms culminating in an agonizing death. All together now, kids. . . .

"Oranges and Lemons": Depending on which historical interpretation you accept, this is about either child sacrifice, public executions, or Henry VIII's marital difficulties. In any case, it ends with the line "Here comes a chopper to chop off your head." So it's not exactly "Little Miss Muffet" (which, in itself, is a rhyme about bloody arachnophobia).

"Georgie Porgie": . . . who "kissed the girls and made them cry" is a charming little ditty about sexual harassment.

"Mary, Mary, Quite Contrary": This is not a song about gardening but a rhyme about homicidal nut job Queen Mary and her taste for torture ("pretty maids all in a row" refers to the newly invented guillotine, and "cockleshells" is apparently a reference to a torture device you attach to the genitals).

These are just a few examples, and there are loads of others.

"Pop Goes the Weasel" is about the cycle of poverty. "Baa, Baa, Black Sheep" is about crippling tax. And "Jack and Jill" is truly horrifying, as it's the name of the worst Adam Sandler film ever made, in which he plays both his sister and himself with "hilarious" consequences. (Actually, "Jack and Jill" is also another one of those catchy, toe-tapping tunes about beheading.)

In fact, in the 1950s a guy called Geoffrey Handley-Taylor, who was worried about all this stuff, studied the two hundred most popular nursery rhymes, and in those he found:

- 8 allusions to murder (unclassified)
- 2 cases of choking to death
- 1 case of cutting a person in half
- 1 case of death by devouring
- 15 allusions to maimed human beings or animals
- 23 cases of physical violence (unclassified)

So, don't worry about playing your kid a bit of thrash death-metal or grime. If your alternative is to expose them to traditional nursery rhymes, you might as well be plopping them down to watch a horror film or someone get torn a new asshole on *Game of Thrones*.

TOYS

When it comes to entertainment, if all else fails you could always try playing with your child.

Play is crucial for your child's social, emotional, physical, and cognitive growth. It's your child's way of learning about his body and the world, and he'll use all five senses to do it, especially in the first year. —BabyCenter.com

So we spent a small fortune on toys that were advertised as educational and engaging: products like Baby Einstein toys that, according to the website, are "designed to enrich baby's young mind." We weren't trying to "hothouse" Charlie or create a genius, but if he could learn something at the same time as he was playing, then that seemed like a good thing. In hindsight, we could have drawn two eyes and a mouth on a cardboard box, and Charlie and "Boxy" would have been friends well into toddlerdom (without the crippling investment in batteries). That's because babies only play in three different ways:

Bash it.
Bite it.
Throw it.

Consequently, when one of Charlie's toys lights up and says in an American accent: "Would you like to learn the ABCs?" Charlie's response is generally: "No, thanks, I think I'm just going to chew your face and repeatedly smash your head against the kitchen floor." Playtime isn't really a time for education as much as a time for destruction-testing cute-looking animatronics. Maybe some of the educational elements go in by osmosis, but whereas we used to measure toys by their educational value, we now measure them by how much punishment they can stand.

The best of Charlie's toys are the immersive ones, the doorway bouncers and ball pools, things like that. The worst of Charlie's toys are the creepy, possessed, battery-devouring toys. The ones with the dead eyes that, out of the blue, with no one anywhere near them, request a hug or ask if you're their friend. In the middle of the night, you hear them turn themselves on and demand to "play," and I sit awake for the next hour trying to hear if they're coming up the stairs or sneakily opening the knife drawer.

And it's not just the ones that turn themselves on that give me the creeps. The most persistently creepy of Charlie's toys is Alfie Bear, who is either singing about how "friendly" he is or insisting that he loves you over and over again like some weird bunny boiler that's terrified you're going to break up with him. To begin with "I love you" is cute; after the four hundredth time, it's just menacing.

Eventually, after many weeks of this creepiness, I couldn't take any more and worked up the courage to take him out into the garden and volley him over the back fence. . . . He was back the following day. Lyns reckons the neighbors found him, but I'm not so sure. I'm not ashamed to say that I'm scared of Alfie Bear. It's with good reason; I'm not a qualified psychiatrist, but from my Googling and observation of Alfie's behavior I'd say that it's possible to give him a significant diagnosis:

SUBJECT: ALFIE BEAR **CASE NOTES 002341:**

Subject suffers from issues related to Low Self-Esteem and may be suffering from a Narcissistic Personality Disorder. If attention is not satisfied, subject shows episodes of Narcissistic Rage expressed as persistent demands to be hugged. Subject also displays compulsive counting behavior indicative of an Obsessive-Compulsive Disorder coupled with excessively repetitive singing, which indicates Attention Hyperactivity. Subject displays little interest in the needs of others and instead is focused entirely on attention-craving and self-interest which may be evidence of sociopathic and possibly psychopathic tendencies.

I mean, you see why I can't bloody sleep with this thing in the house.

Generally, I'm concerned about the influence that these toys are having on Charlie, and despite the fact that most professionals contend that interactive toys are great for your baby, I'm not convinced. Scientists might argue that TV is bad, but no one is saying a great deal about the flashing lights of the singing, dancing psychopaths wandering around our living room.

And here's a scary question: What happens if we don't want to be friends?

Thankfully, Charlie seems to have got bored with, or grown out of, a lot of his most annoying toys, and he no longer has any interest in Alfie Bear (who remains buried at the bottom of the toy box, like a Manchurian candidate waiting to be reactivated). As babies get more curious and active, their taste in toys seems to change rapidly. When Charlie was about six months old, his favorite toys were Alfie, a pull-along telephone, and some stacking blocks. Now that he is older, crawling, and more curious, his top ten favorite toys are more eclectic. This week's top ten chart of "Shit That Charlie Likes to Play With" is as follows:

10. Any cupboard door or drawer. (Open door or drawer. Insert fingers. Close door or drawer on fingers. Melt the f*ck down. Repeat.)
9. The eyes or nose of any close relative (clawing and/or gouging)
8. The oven door (only when oven is on)
7. The dog's water bowl
6. The dog's food bowl
5. The dog's tail
4. The dog's wafer-thin sanity
3. Cups of tea or coffee . . . and anything else dangerously hot
2. Dropping to number 2 in this week's chart after a long run at the top: Power outlets (exploring with drool-wet fingers)
1. And a brand-new entry, straight in at number 1: The kitchen garbage can (for some reason, he suddenly likes licking it)

PLAYTIME

To be honest, when it comes to playtime, all toys are pale shadows of the things that delight babies the most. And what keeps babies entranced more than anything are those things that are individual to you and your little family. For example, Charlie enjoys it when Lyndsay pretends that he is a giant baby attacking a city, or when I pretend to be a robot sent from the future to crush his tiny head. He also never fails to laugh at the baby in the mirror we call "Barry," or when I just pretend to fall asleep and snore and wake up as the Hulk. You get the idea. These are just a few of a hundred and one stupid games we play that mean nothing to anyone outside of us three. All families have their own uniquely daft games that captivate both parents and baby. And it is the uniqueness of these games that is the finest reminder that your little person is an individual from the very start.

It is also in these bits of nonsense that entertaining your little one is at its simple best. Because good parents are the "toys" that are willing to tailor themselves to their baby's character and brand-new personality. In the end, there isn't a teddy bear, train set, or stack of blocks that can compete.

EXTERNAL ACTIVITIES

If you're against TV and think books are for bedtime, you're worried about the effect of gangsta rap, or you're just concerned that one of your child's dead-eyed toys is thinking about stabbing you in your sleep, it may be time to consider entertainment outside the home.

The scale of the industry built up around attempting to entertain your new arrival is astonishing and expensive. In the past, activities for babies were restricted to pushing junior down to the shops when you'd run out of smokes. Nowadays, though, there is a mind-bending array of classes to choose from: you have the option of baby yoga, baby sign language, baby sensory, swim babies . . . and probably baby tree-felling and baby deep-sea fishing, etc.

These are just some of the activities we've tried over the past year:

Baby sign language

This seemed like a good idea. I'd seen it in a film once, a baby before it could talk, signing that it was hungry or tired. Actually, now that I think about it, it might not have been a baby (it was a bit hairier than that)—it might have been a gorilla or a chimp or something. Anyway, the principle is the same. To begin with, babies are in a preverbal stage of their development, so if you can teach them some basic sign language, they can tell you if they're cold, hungry, or tired. And so, for five weeks, I spent every Thursday afternoon sitting on my ass in a damp church hall with seven women, all trying to learn the sign language for *poop*.

This is where it collapsed. I had to learn the signs first so that I could then teach them to Charlie. Unfortunately, I'm an idiot and have the memory of timber. And, while Charlie's brain might be a sponge, my brain is more of a petrified rock of dinosaur shit, no more capable of taking in useful information than an upturned bucket. If you throw the necessity for hand–eye coordination into that mix, it's a disaster. By the time I was trying to pass the sign language I'd learned on to Charlie, I was pretty much guessing.

And so when I believed I was teaching Charlie the sign for *milk*:

I was actually teaching him the sign for *bowling*:

And when I was sure I was teaching him the sign for *hungry*:

he was actually learning the slightly less useful sign for *tractor*:

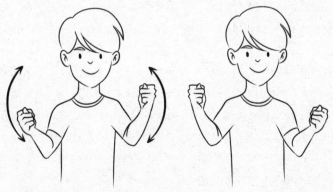

So after five weeks, we stopped going.

. . . For the simple reason that, after more than a month, Charlie, through no fault of his own, had learned nothing. And in the unlikely event that he found himself relying on his knowledge of sign language in order to survive, he would have dehydrated and starved to death. As he repeatedly demanded to go bowling on a tractor.

Baby rave

This is what it sounds like. It is exactly the same as an adult rave, except everyone in attendance is four feet shorter and more likely to lose their shit when a balloon bursts.

In fact, in a lot of ways, a baby rave is much better than an adult rave. Okay, the music is just as shit, but: Hardly anyone tries to sell you ketamine. You don't have to meet off the freeway near Fresno to find out where it's going to be. And you haven't got some idiot in white gloves, with a glow stick and a whistle, flailing his arms and elbowing you in the face every two minutes just because the DJ's started to play something by Basshunter.

A real plus is that baby raves tend to be organized for the morning. So it's all done and dusted by lunchtime and you can go home for a nice cup of tea.

Boom.

Actually, I really do recommend a good baby rave. From what I've seen, the older kids love it—the flashing lights, the smoke, and the bassy music—and the younger kids love watching the older kids loving it.

And watching how the parents behave in this environment is interesting: from the uncomfortable mom shuffling with a baby in her arms to the "Big fish, little fish, cardboard box" dad-dancing, this is all a great reminder that your coolness is swallowed up by parenthood. But it is also a reminder of what you're missing from your clubbing days: absolutely nothing.

ENTERTAINMENT

Baby sensory

Baby sensory classes are designed to fire the five senses of your baby: sight, smell, touch, hearing, and biting. These classes bombard babies with sound and light. Part disco, part puppet show, part singsong, part sign-language instruction, they feature tambourines, maracas, bubbles, balloons, inflatable animals . . . and a song in which you say hello to sweet corn. If you've got a baby who's easily bored, it's great, because for about an hour they have a "shock and awe" bombardment of sensory stimulation thrown at them.

The local one we go to is awesome, but completely dizzying. Each class has so much glitter and sparkle and disco lighting that it feels as though you've wandered into RuPaul's brain and he's planning the opening ceremony of a gay-pride Olympics.

The lady who runs our class goes by the name of Crazy Claire. Which is an apt name. I'm pretty sure she's not actually mad (I mean, she might keep body parts in her freezer for all I know, but, to be fair, she doesn't seem the type). She is, though, one of the most enthusiastic people I've ever met, and it's infectious.

The first class we went to, I was quietly tapping away with a tambourine, feeling pretty awkward. I wasn't really sure what was going on, as everyone else joined in songs about sunshine and being friends. And Charlie looked equally unsure. But by the third class, we were carried away by Crazy Claire's enthusiasm, and I found myself rowing along in an invisible boat, surrounded by bubbles and balloons, singing something about pirates, and bashing on an upturned plastic tub like I was in *Stomp*. I still don't know why and it doesn't matter. That's not the point. It's fun.

I would definitely recommend baby sensory to anybody looking to entertain their little one. It's true that, to begin with, it feels like you've stumbled into some strange therapy session after ingesting handpicked mushrooms.

But there is method in the madness. In fact, the method *is* the madness. The great thing about baby sensory is its relentless unexpectedness. For an hour, it is an ever-changing environment. Always interesting. For babies, it is like all the good bits of TV, the attention-grabbing color and sound and light, without being reduced to two dimensions and trapped in a little box. Charlie is enthralled by it because there is no time to get bored with one activity before you are onto the next. And for a creature with the attention span of a cod, that's ideal.

Messy play

The first rule of messy play is: you don't talk about messy play.

The second rule of messy play is—what am I talking about? There are no rules.

It's demented.

Okay, when it comes to kids, there's no such thing as "tidy play." From what I've seen, it doesn't matter what age they are, all preadults can turn a perfectly clean and tidy room into a scene of devastation in a matter of seconds. (I remember babysitting for my nephew once. I left the room for one minute and returned to discover he'd crayoned all over the TV, the walls, and the carpet. When I asked what on earth he'd done, he just held up a piece of paper with a crazy scrawl on it and said: "A picture of a cat.")

So all play is messy, but when you introduce paint, foam, pasta, glue, and glitter, and you remove all rules? You are inviting Armageddon.

I don't know whether all messy plays are the same, but the one that we go to? There really are no rules. It's just poster paint, shaving foam, flour, and water, and Christ knows what else, all dumped onto a massive plastic mat. On arrival you just strip your baby down to his diaper and slide him into the mix like he is trying to win a Walkman on J. D. Roth's *Fun House*. (If you were born after 1985, ask your parents.) Unlike the other activities we do, there's no real structure to messy play; the closest thing we got to it at our local class was a different "painting" exercise each week.

There was:

"Painting a Picture": which was eating paint, while sitting in paint.

"Handprint Painting": which was eating paint, while sitting in paint.

And "Potato-Print Painting": which was eating paint, while sitting in paint. With a potato nearby.

Six-month-old babies . . . not big painters.

The hardest bit about messy play is obviously the cleanup. Thankfully, you don't have to clean up the actual mess, because that's what you pay your three dollars for. But it is with a heavy heart that you end every session with the painful realization that you are responsible for your own offspring. (It is tempting to just grab the cleanest one and raise that one as your own.) And before you can even contemplate cleaning your own baby, you have to unstick your particular offspring from the block of babies now in the middle of the room. Since during playtime they've got all stuck together like Whoppers left in a hot car. Once they're separated, it's hard to describe the resultant effects of messy play on your baby. How bad it is. It's a bit like you've coated them in glue and rolled them around on a landfill site.

It's heaven for Charlie. He loves being messy, and this is a short window of time when he can be. A time when he isn't being persistently wiped clean, the thing he detests most in the world.

It's quite sad that as adults we have largely forgotten the simple joy and abandon of all this mayhem (the closest I have been to adult messy play was sharing a kebab-house table with a bachelorette night in Newcastle). But there is fun to be had in seeing your child's delight in being grotesquely filthy—and besides, unless you turn up with a haz-mat suit and baby-sized tongs, you're going to get pretty messy yourself. There's no way of avoiding it.

Just one word of advice: if the baby's grandparents are looking after the little one the following day, mention to them that there's a chance that your baby may have ingested a load of multicolored poster paint and glitter. Otherwise, they may spend two hours on the phone to Poison Control in a panic, inquiring as to why junior might be shitting rainbows.

Baby yoga

I'll admit, I went to this one accidentally. I got the wrong day for baby sign language and turned up at the community center on a Wednesday morning rather than a Thursday.

Rather than do the sensible thing—apologize for intruding, turn 180 degrees, and head off for a bacon sandwich—I pretended I was in exactly the right place. I paid my five dollars and embarked on my only foray into the world of yoga. It was a disaster. Not least because Charlie slept through the entire class.

It is the only time I have felt uncomfortable being the only male participant in a baby activity class. But, I think, with good reason. There is something inherently uncomfortable about being in a class of fourteen Lycra-clad moms (each with her alert baby, yoga ball, and mat) when you are the only man, your baby is fast asleep, and you are sitting there in jeans and a cardigan . . . unconvincingly trying to strengthen your postbirth pelvic floor.

We didn't go back. I suspect as much to their relief as mine.

Baby swimming

Personally, I can't remember learning how to swim. I just always could. I must have been taught how, I just don't remember. In fact, my abiding recollections of swimming as a kid are often haunted by a memory of competing in a swimming meet when I was about nine. I was in a race with six other kids, and we were being cheered on by Richard Ogden's granddad, who was running along the side of the pool in his trunks. I remember this extremely clearly because the old man obviously had no idea that he had one testicle hanging out of the side of his Speedos. (I can only imagine that while he was excitedly cheering us on, this ancient ball had worked its way loose.)

Needless to say, I didn't win the race. In fact, I think I came in last. I was quite a good swimmer but just couldn't concentrate on the finish line with that thing winking at me from the side of the pool like a parched baked potato.

Despite this, on the whole, my memories of spending days and weeks of summer vacation at the local pool are times that I look back on with great nostalgia: the dive-bombing, the hold-your-breath contests, the "no running" walk-run, the fights over plastic floats, the local pervert, "Colin," and his tendency to sit underwater in the shallow end with his goggles on.

Even memories of the after-swim ritual of chips and a cola from the vending machine evoke feelings of a simpler time when I used to sit around in the café with Paul Johnston arguing about what "heavy petting" might be, before strolling home feeling the effects of the 90 percent chlorine we'd been swimming in (as if we had collective conjunctivitis or were on our way back from a G20 protest where we'd been teargassed by cops).

We didn't know each other at the time, but me and Lyns actually grew up about two hundred yards from one another. I think we didn't know each other when we were children simply because boys smell and girls are crazy. We do, though, both have fond memories of our local pool, and we like to think that, although we can't remember it, we used to scrap over floats and dive-bomb near each other.

It was partly this nostalgia that made us so keen to take Charlie to swimming classes. It would be great to think that he would come to enjoy the childhood friendships and fun of swimming as much as we did during our long summer vacation. (Minus Colin and the potato.)

Plus, it struck us as common sense to make sure that he was safe around water. (And if we could get him to swim underwater and re-create the *Nevermind* album cover, then so much the better. Loads of people I've spoken to got interested in their baby swimming purely because of that cover. Which seems a strange legacy for a tortured soul like Kurt Cobain. Maybe if he'd known he would make such a great contribution to infant water safety, he wouldn't have been such a Debbie Downer.) So we enrolled in baby swimming classes as soon as Charlie was old enough.

As it happens, baby "swimming" is a bit of a misnomer as, to begin with, it's not so much swimming as "nondrowning."

Most animals—cats, dogs, monkeys, even pigs—are born with the ability to swim, but humans aren't. Before our first class, I was suffering from the common misconception that babies are natural swimmers. I was wrong. Lesson number one: babies sink.

Babies do have something called a bradycardic response, though, which basically means that they instinctively hold their breath when underwater. Which is useful, because, to begin with, handling your baby in water can be tricky. It's quite alarming how often you feel the need to sidle up to someone in your swimming class who is accidentally holding their baby beneath the waterline. (It's an awkward tap on the shoulder when you have to follow it up with: "Er, excuse me, sorry to bother you, but your baby's drowning.")

So at this age, babies (or at least those in the newborns' class) don't swim. There are no tiny six-month-olds doing laps and tumble-turning as they switch from the crawl to the butterfly.

Instead, baby "swimming lessons" are largely made up of exercises that involve sing-alongs and splishing and splashing, holding on to the side of the pool, and other simple routines that are designed to get your baby accustomed to being in the water without fear.

Then there are the more weird exercises. Like the one that involves placing your little one on a float and pushing him away from the side of the pool. An exercise that makes it feel like you're committing your child to a Viking burial at sea. (The first time we did this, I half expected a flaming arrow to come flying over my shoulder and set the whole thing on fire.)

But apart from the exercises that teach water safety and those that are evocative of sending your baby on a noble fiery path toward Valhalla, the hardest exercise is the "underwater swim."

Again, these aren't really swims. It is more dunking than swimming. The first time they "underwater swim," it amounts to you saying, "Ready, steady, go," and then plunging the baby underwater like a donut into coffee, before scooping him back up again. And if you think that this would freak a baby out . . . you'd be right, as when he reappears he tends to do so coughing and spluttering and with a confused look in his eyes directed at you that says: "What the fuck are you doing, you idiot??"

It's tough, that first time. That look of panic and confusion. But it's amazing how quickly babies get used to the idea of being dunked and even start to enjoy it. In the beginning, it's difficult to shake the feeling that you're doing something against your better instincts—the tiny seconds that they spend beneath the water feel like an age.

But Charlie now enjoys swimming more than anything else. And after several months of classes, he has no fear of water and is even starting to propel himself through the pool like an incredibly slow and wayward torpedo. Strangely, one of the main things he enjoys is drinking the pool water. At home, we can't get him to drink more than two sips from a sippy cup (it just gloobles everywhere like he's had novocaine); but put him in a pool that is 50 percent baby pee and 50 percent chemicals, and he glugs it like it's Fanta. Though the thing he really enjoys is the other kids, the way they splash each other and shout in the echoes of the pool area. And as long as he enjoys all that, we'll put up with the suspiciously warm water and keep on dunking.

The Penistone and District Historical Society

The Penistone and District Historical Society is a group of twelve retired men and women who get together every Tuesday morning, at a community center near where I live, to chat about the history of my village, Penistone.

Okay, so, I got the wrong fucking day again. But the historical society members were lovely, we had homemade lemonade and cookies, I found out why the Penistone train no longer runs to Broadbottom or Gorton, and I also won some deodorant in their weekly raffle.

*   *   *

So, if you're keeping score: baby sensory, swimming, raving, messy play, and the Penistone and District Historical Society's weekly meeting are all great ways to entertain your baby away from home. Baby sign language is okay (if you have the patience and brains for it), and baby yoga is shit.

And none of them get even close to peekaboo.

THE CURTAIN

It's hard work entertaining a baby. And for what? We are told that it's important for cognitive development and the familial bonding process, or whatever. But the payoff isn't in educational attainment or development; it is in a baby's chuckle or smile. And if you think that sounds like something Oprah would say, it's actually science, you cynical shit. Studies show that a baby's smile and giggle activate areas in the parent's brain like the "striatum" and the "ventral tegmental" (and other complicated bits of the brain with names that sound like Harry Potter casting spells), and these are the oddly named bits in your skull that apparently light up like a pinball machine when you're happy.

So as parents I think it's best to get happy. And activate our "ventral tegmental" while we can. For now, the fact that I disappear when I hide behind my hands makes me a great magician. But it will not be long before Charlie realizes that I never disappeared at all, that I was there all along. Just as one day he will realize that I don't have the ability to produce a coin from behind his ear, and that I haven't snatched his nose but simply tucked my thumb behind my forefinger.

So we'll get down on all fours, make faces for all we're worth, and peekaboo like fuck. And bask in the glowing reviews of our little one's smile. Because one day the spell will be broken, the curtain pulled back, and our career as the greatest entertainer in our child's life will be over. Forever.

9

MILESTONES

It's incredible how a baby's milestones mirror those of human evolution. Just as in our prehistory, when our ancestors were formed in a primordial soup, took their first infant crawl onto land, and learned a basic grunting communication before finding the ability to walk upright.

So, too, babies leave the alchemy of the womb behind to take the same evolutionary steps: the ability to crawl, walk, and talk, and all in their first months of life.

. . . Actually, now that I think about it, as incredible as it is that a baby's milestones are the same as the evolution of man, I'm really hoping that those milestones stop being so similar. Because the next steps for man were to discover fire, learn how to use a spear, and fuck over the nearest tribe for their women and livestock.

MILESTONES

Dear Charlie,

So, it occurs to me that one day you will be all grown up and you might actually read this book. (Maybe you'll discover it in an old bookshop or, if nobody buys it, you might stumble across one of the twenty thousand copies we keep in the garage.)

With that in mind, I thought, in this penultimate chapter, I'd take this opportunity to tell you a bit more about what you were like during your first 365-day orbit around the sun. Take this chance to tell you how you met your milestones, those little markers by the road that define the first year of all of our lives. How you made your first word, your first step, things like that.

Sit up straight.

MILESTONE NO. 1:
HOW YOU GOT YOUR NAME

So, when your mom was pregnant, we went along to the hospital for a six-month scan. This is the scan when the nurse can detect whether the parents are having a boy or a girl. We didn't want to know. We wanted you to be a surprise. You don't get many surprises as an adult, and when you do they tend to be shit, like a speeding ticket or jury duty or a suspicious lump. It's not like being a kid when everything is good-surprising, so we kept this one for ourselves. And to be honest, at the time, we didn't care whether you were going to be a boy or a girl anyway.

(I know everybody says that, but we really didn't care. At an earlier scan, the same nurse asked me directly whether I preferred a boy or a girl, and I trotted out the stock response, which is: "I don't mind, as long as the baby's healthy." And that's genuinely the way I felt. But this particular nurse was quite pushy; she said: "Oh, everyone says that! What if I could wave a magic wand, what would you want?" So I thought, and then told her: "I would probably go for something with Professor X's mind, but with Wolverine's healing capabilities." She just looked at me like I was insane. I thought: *Christ, you're the one with the magic wand, love. . . .*).

Anyway, the scanning nurse covered up any telltale (or tell-tail) signs of whether you were a boy or a girl, and you remained neither boy nor girl until the day you landed.

Because we chose not to find out whether you would be a junior or a junioress, our first milestone was to give you a name. Deciding on a name before you got here was awkward—we didn't really want to settle on "Bernard" or "Troy," only to discover that we had a little princess on our hands. Likewise, we didn't want to set our hearts on "Penelope," and find that we had a little boy (who, if you were to take after your mom's dad, would grow to be a six-foot-four man, with hands like shovels and a build that calls to mind a brick shithouse).

I don't think it's just us who have had this problem. I think, for a lot of parents, naming their little one is quite difficult. Even if parents-to-be decide to find out the sex of their baby (or are organized enough to set aside options for both boy and girl), it's not necessarily straightforward to find a name that both mom and dad agree on. It's a strange thing about names: we attach associations to them, both positive and negative, and we do it all the time. For example, if your school bully is called "Glen," it's unlikely you'll want to give your firstborn the same name. And if the girl who first broke your heart was named "Sally," likewise you won't want to be reminded of that each time you call your kid to dinner. The problem is, your partner's school bully might have been called "Frank," and the person who broke their heart was "Terry." So you fast start to run out of names that are agreeable.

Because of these random associations we make to names, me and your mom started to have conversations like this:

"What about Mark?"

"No, sounds like a dentist."

"What about Jason?"

"No, sounds like a piss-head."

"What about Sarah?"

"No, sounds like the sort of girl who would get her friends to tell you that she fancies you, just so that when you ask her if she wants to go Rollerblading, she can humiliate you by saying no in front of the entire school cafeteria. Then, to add insult to injury, start rumors about you, saying that you shit yourself during PE (when you didn't, you just sat in some hot chocolate). And then you're the one who gets in trouble for carving her name into a desk with the words 'Die, Sarah, die.'"

Y'know, er . . . conversations like that.

So when it came to giving you a name, we got a bit stuck. Naming you felt like giving you a bearing, it felt like we were placing a flag in the earth that said: "This new person is here, he is part of our community of humans, and with this name you can mark him as worthy of title." So it seemed quite important to get it right.

Strangely, as soon as you arrived and we found out that you were a little boy, we settled on the name Charlie pretty quickly. (You have to decide pretty quickly after the birth; otherwise you're calling the baby "the baby" all the time.)

In hindsight, it seems that we'd actually been circling around the name before you got here. Charlie was your great-grandpa's name, and he was a good man. Dependable, hardworking, and about as cheerfully Irish as you can get without straying into leprechaun territory. And it seemed a solid idea to continue a family tradition.

Don't get me wrong—I know some people are insistent on giving their babies traditional family names, but it wasn't like that. Naming you after my granddad wasn't a line in the sand. We liked the name as well. If my granddad had been called Jedediah Fuckfingers the Third, we probably would have gone for something else. But when it came down to it, Charlie seemed like the name of someone who was kind and lucky and a good friend.

What is really strange, though, is that after all the talk and agonizing about names, when we finally gave you yours, it felt a lot like we hadn't named you at all. It felt more like it was what you had always been called, and we had just uncovered it somehow.

So we hope you like it.

If you don't, tough.

Just keep in mind that it could have been worse. You could have been born to a celebrity and called North or Apple, for example. (Good luck going to school in the industrial heartlands of Yorkshire when you're named after a fruit or a point of the compass.) And if you think that's bad, there was a piece in the newspaper, the same week you were born, about other dodgy names that parents have given their kids. I made a note of some of the names from that article. They include:

- Monkey
- Ninja Qwest
- Vejonica
- Sex Fruit
- Phelony
- Chairish
- Brfxxccxxmnpcccclllmmnprxvclmnckssqlbb11116 (pronounced "Albin")
- Uteraz
- Yr Hyness
- Punched
- Horse Dick
- Mafia No Fear
- Anus
- Robocop

So, if for whatever reason you're not a fan of the name Charlie, suck it up—you could have been called Robocop Horse Dick Coyne.

MILESTONE NO. 2: YOUR FIRST SMILE

So then you were here, name and all. And I think your entrance is pretty well covered in Chapter 1. (Don't let that put you off having kids. It's worth every "red in tooth and claw" moment. And besides, when it comes to childbirth, you won the lottery—you're a man. All you have to do is turn up with change for the parking spot and keep an expression on your face that suggests you know what the fuck is going on.)

In the very moment of your arrival, it was pretty clear that your mom loved you immediately, unconditionally, and without any reservation. But you and me? For the first few days, we eyed each other quite suspiciously.

Don't get me wrong, I loved you too, but you were quite boring. Nothing personal—all newborns are pretty boring. After the adrenaline of labor and coming home subsides, it's a bit like finding a jellyfish washed up on the beach: once you've looked at it for a bit and poked it with a stick, you find out that it doesn't do a lot.

And, because you didn't do a lot, it was quite hard for me to get a handle on who you were.

When I look back now, the first sense of that handle was in this milestone: your first smile.

There isn't a great deal to write about it, other than to say that the first time you did smile, it was something momentous.

I once did a ball-achingly boring school project on a Victorian intellectual called John Ruskin. The only thing I can remember about it was something he said about penguins. He said: "One can't be angry when one looks at a penguin."

He might as well have been talking about your smile, and while that might sound sentimental, and you may be reading this as a teenager with rolling eyes and saying to the page: "God, Dad, that is so embarrassing," I don't care. Maybe one day you will have a kid of your own, or maybe you already have one and you have found out for yourself: your own baby's smile is a firework. A thing so powerful that it is almost like armor. A defense for a creature without defense.

You first smiled at around two weeks. Experts, baby professionals, pediatricians—they will all tell you that newborn babies don't smile, and certainly not at two weeks. They will insist that babies don't start smiling until they are around two months old and that, before then, it is just a reflex or a sign that they are passing wind. But the first time you smiled, I knew what all parents know: that when it comes to this, experts are full of shit.

You did smile. And rather than accept the perceived wisdom that it was impossible, we came to the conclusion that anyone who tried to tell us otherwise was wrong and trying to deprive us of something magical, and that those people were bitter, twisted, joy-thieving fuckfaces who make Darth Maul look like Ellen DeGeneres.

You smiled.

It was a Sunday night, and we'd just taken you out of the bath and were drying you on your changing table. Your mom was singing: "Jump, jump went the little green frog." Which is a song about a frog whose eyes go "blink, blink, blink." And I was attempting to distract you by doing the "actions" over your mom's shoulder (these were mainly facial expressions that I thought looked a lot like a frog, but which your mom cruelly told me looked a lot more like Andrew Lloyd Webber's sex face).

It's impossible to know why (and you will never remember and be able to let us know), but this combination of weird sounds and making faces fired something like amusement in your tiny brain. You momentarily focused on us both and smiled: first with an up-curve of your lips and then with your eyes. And your mom happy-cried (she was doing that a lot then) and we celebrated. We needed it: at the time, we were as knackered as we would ever be.

So, as a milestone, your first smile was an important one for all of us. At a point when we were struggling with how high-maintenance and what a massive pain in the ass a baby was turning out to be, it was a transference of energy, a reviver, and a moment when I thought: *You know what? This kid's all right.*

MILESTONE NO. 3: YOUR FIRST TOOTH

You weren't born with teeth. Which I'm quite glad about. Apparently some babies are, which must be quite bizarre. Teeth seem a specifically non-newborn accessory, like a beard or a pipe.

The only reason I was worried about this was that I'd read somewhere about a baby from the UK who was born with ten of his teeth, all there and ready to chew. And I was a bit weirded out by the idea of you arriving, and gazing up at us for the first time to reveal a grille of Simon Cowell–esque gnashers. (I worried about the strangest things before you were born, but I'm guessing your mom was even more pleased that you didn't arrive like that. I don't think any mom would be that keen on breast-feeding a newborn that looks like it could make short work of a stick of rock candy.)

Anyway, for most babies, teeth appear at about four months, and your first one appeared as timetabled and it was a moment of relief. Not least because it demonstrated some sort of progress through the trials of teething.

Before you were born, I'd heard parents constantly explain away their children's crying, screaming, and tantrums with the excuse that their little one was teething. In my pathetic ignorance, I probably thought that it was just an excuse for their baby being a grouch.

Especially since babies always seemed to be teething. When my friends' kid's crying was excused away for the twentieth time that month with "It's his teeth coming through," I used to think: *Jesus, how many teeth is this kid going to have? It's a baby, not a shark.*

But, in reality, it's not making excuses at all. Cutting teeth is brutal and can take ages. Days and weeks of pain for just one stubborn tooth to force its appearance. The experience of seeing the pain you felt during the arrival of your first tooth was a lesson in my ignorance and stupidity, and it was a lesson well learned.

The classic signs were there, that your first tooth was on its way, a good two weeks before it could even be seen. You were slavering like a Saint Bernard staring into a butcher's shop window, and you had the telltale flushed cheeks, the bright crimson of a drunk gnome. And that's exactly what you looked like, minus a stupid hat, a fishing rod, a toadstool to sit on, and any hint of cheeriness.

As this first tooth started to push through, you were miserable. All you wanted to do was chew. To put my or your mom's finger or thumb in your mouth and bite down with angry gums. Until one painful day when a razor-sharp shred of enamel cut through and your mom realized too late that she had her finger in a human pencil sharpener.

It soon became clear that offering you a teether was preferable to having our fingers chomped on or allowing you to gnaw on a table leg or a stray electrical cord. So we bought you all shapes and sizes (simple rings full of gel that could be frozen, and others in the shape of a giraffe or a set of keys), and you sat on our laps as you forced through those early teeth by chewing away on these things like a rabid puppy with a pigskin shoe.

Usually, the first teeth to arrive are the bottom two. The cutesy little Tic Tacs that you see in the smiles that grace baby magazines. But your first teeth were the top two canines. The vampire teeth. Which were pointy and made you look like Count Orlok or one of the Lost Boys. For a while, it was difficult to tell whether you were upset because you were teething or because you didn't like direct sunlight or garlic and were hankering for the blood of the innocent.

As a milestone, the first tooth wasn't a very enjoyable one. It was hard watching you get your first tooth and, for that matter, all the rest of them. You no doubt can't remember the discomfort, but if you've experienced toothache since you will know that it is one of the most excruciating things you can endure. It was heart-shredding at times when you were coping with the pain of teething and the accompanying fever and chills and you couldn't express that pain in a way that we could make it better.

So teething is crap, but when a new smile came with your first tooth, it was a bonus milestone. A moment that seemed like real progress and a twinkling that felt like we were dealing with a little person, developing a character and growing fast. And, yes, for a while when you smiled, you looked like a cross between Nosferatu and Blade, but for three months you were our little vampire, and you looked badass.

So, sunshine, look after your teeth. Cut down on the sugary drinks and cookies, and brush and floss twice daily. Because I don't know about the ones you have now, but the first lot you had, they took some getting.

MILESTONE NO. 4:
CRAWLING

Apparently, babies are supposed to start crawling at about seven or eight months old. But you took your time. Each week we went to one of your activity classes (like baby sensory or whatever), and we were surrounded by little kiddies of about the same age as you, and they all seemed to be tear-assing around on their bellies like windup toys: little giddy soldiers commando-crawling all over the place. You just kind of sat there and watched, occasionally rolling on your back and staring up at the ceiling for a bit. You could see all these kids crawling around, but had no interest in doing the same. You looked at them like they were idiots, and they looked at you like you were the class stoner.

You were like your dad: lazy. But you'd also got it sussed out. If there was something you wanted, and it was a few feet away, you'd just grab the rug it was on and pull it toward yourself like you were reeling in a fish. Or you'd just stare at something and jabber until someone fetched it for you. In a lot of ways, you behaved as though crawling was beneath you.

In the end, one day we decided to stop fetching you stuff. And, after a couple of weeks of you looking at us like we were slaves who had revolted, it started to work.

Eventually you seemed to get bored of waiting for things to magically appear in your hands and you started rolling toward them. Then, after a while, you started to shuffle and shimmy on your stomach, coordinate your arms and legs, and slowly but surely move . . . backward.

You mastered going backward pretty quickly. For weeks, you couldn't move forward at all, but you could reverse under the settee with remarkable speed and efficiency. This reversing wasn't deliberate, though, and it created its own frustration. You could see the place you were trying to get to, but the more frantically you tried to get there, the more your brain ballsed the whole thing up and made you reverse away from it. (That's got to be pretty annoying; I'm sure there's a metaphor for life or something in there.)

And with this frustration as the catalyst, you started to crawl. Sort of.

To begin with, it was slow and it wasn't pretty. But if anybody needed a small object that was less than three feet away, and had a good hour to wait . . . you were the man.

We checked your progress on the NHS website, which said that there were three stages to learning to crawl that we should be aware of; but for you, from beginning to full crawling, there were about six.

Stage 1. The Plank: Basically, we'd put you down on your front and you would just lie there motionless. (It was only your breathing that told us that you were still actually alive.) Your uncle Paul suggested we try you on a different surface, so we tried you in the garden rather than on a carpet. But you still didn't move. You just lay there face-down on the grass, as if you'd just jumped out of a plane and your parachute had failed to open.

Stage 2. Tummy Time: This was the same as The Plank, apart from the vaguest of movements. Your legs kicked a bit, but to be honest, you were mostly just licking the floor.

Stage 3. The Inverted Turtle: By now, we could put you down, and while you still wouldn't crawl, your head would pop up and your arms and legs would start to windmill, a bit like an enthusiastic bath toy deprived of water.

Stage 4. The Carpet Hump: Lots of backward motion, some attempted forward motion, but, yeah, you were mainly just humping the carpet.

Stage 5. The Zombie Drag: And then you were crawling! You were never going to win any land-speed records, and you did look a bit like one of those legless zombies off *The Walking Dead*, dragging itself over a train track. But you had come a long way in a short space of time, and we couldn't have been more proud.

After a few days, though, you'd really got the hang of it and we began to wonder why the living fuck we had ever been so desperate for you to crawl in the first place . . .

Stage 6. The Horror: Okay, as much as we were delighted that you had begun to crawl, once you'd really got the hang of it, it was terrifying. You were like one of those face-huggers from *Aliens* skittering around the place. If we turned our backs for a second, you were gone, seemingly always heading toward the most dangerous thing in the room.

Until that point, I'd never noticed what a death trap our house was, and flush with the success of your newfound skill, you thought yourself an explorer, curious and invincible: "Ooh, there's a sharp corner of a piece of furniture, I think I'll go and impale my eye on that"; "Ooh, there's an electric outlet over there, I'd better lick my fingers and stick them in it like it's a fucking bowling ball." It was/is a nightmare. You never stay in the same place for more than a matter of seconds—when you're not messing with outlets, you're emptying drawers and bookshelves or stuffing pulped breakfast cereal into the disc drive of the PlayStation.

(I'm going to stop writing there for a second, because two minutes ago you were playing around my feet and now you've disappeared into the kitchen, no doubt to hang off of the oven door or lick the side of the trash can. . . . You do that.)

MILESTONE NO. 5:
YOUR FIRST WORDS

The hardest thing about you starting to burble and make chatty noises was that your mom enforced a rule in the house that there would no longer be any swearing. It made sense. We didn't want you wandering into school at four years old with the vocabulary of a pissed-off construction worker.

"Morning, Charlie, how are you today?"

"Fucking spot-on, Miss Jenkins."

So it made sense to tackle this problem early, before you started talking properly. The problem is that I casually swear quite a lot, so for me this was quite hard. Hopefully by the time you read this, I've widened my own vocabulary and successfully curbed my potty mouth. But as it stands, in this your first year, I have a tendency to swear like Gordon Ramsay with his penis trapped in a car door.

It was at your mom's suggestion that we introduced a swear jar. And it was only with the introduction of the jar that I realized how persistent my bad language is. Complying with the jar, I was almost permanently broke from putting in fifty cents every time I uttered an expletive. So in the end, to avoid personal bankruptcy, I negotiated with your mom for a sliding scale of fines:

Months after its introduction, I'm continuing to keep up with the swear jar, and it's actually proving to be quite a positive thing. Don't get me wrong, I still swear just as much as I did, but at the rate I'm going, by the time you read this there will be enough in the jar to buy you your first house.

So when you did start to talk, it was some relief that your first words weren't in any way offensive.

It was June 24, in the same week as Father's Day, and you said the word "Daddy."

Okay, it wasn't exactly your first word: for months you had been saying words like "weeeelk," "bumder," "oddjob," "Barry," and something that sounded a bit like "muung-beeaans."

. . . And for weeks before that you'd been calling your mom "Bob."

But on June 24, when you first said "Daddy," at that point you still hadn't said "Mommy," and that was a big deal in our house.

I'm not going to lie. It was a hard-fought, sometimes underhanded battle for whether you would say "Mommy" or "Daddy" first. It was a cold war. Your mom tried to get you to call me Matt rather than Dad and repeated the words "Mom Mom Mom" to you, over and over and at every opportunity. For my campaign, I repeated the word "Daddy" over and over. But I also took advantage of the fact that some of your favorite toys had a function on them that allowed you to record your own voice. And I went round each of them, loading them up with "Dad Dad Dad" in an attempt to imprint it on your brain. Basically, we both used the finest traditions of North Korean brain-rinsing to try to get you to say "Mom" or "Dad" first.

And I won.

In fairness, babies often say "Daddy" first. Apparently, it's easier for their mouths to form the word. And, knowing this and understanding that defeat would be tough on your mom, I tried to be sensitive to her feelings. It's always best to accept victory with grace and humility.

So I restricted my celebrations to just a few dignified laps around the house, with you on my shoulders, singing "We Are the Champions," and an hour or so of pointing at your mom and chanting: "Who arrre yer? Who are yer?" etc., while she sat and ate her dinner.

We also drew her a little picture to cheer her up.

MILESTONE NO. 6:
YOUR FIRST STEPS

Well, this is awkward.

Believe it or not, I wrote a rough plan for this book. I'm just looking at it now. The plan was to cover the first year, and it was at this point that I was going to write about when you started walking. What it was like when you hit this defining first-year milestone. The big one: your first steps.

Only thing is, as I write this, you're not walking. In fact, you've not taken any steps at all. First or otherwise. And you turn one year old tomorrow.

So, thanks a lot, Charlie boy, book ruined.

Or maybe not.

I've just spoken to my mom, your nan, and she tells me that it was always unlikely that you were ever going to be walking by the time you were one. Apparently, most kids don't start walking until well after they're a year old. In fact, she also tells me that *I* didn't start walking until I was eighteen months. "You really were a lazy sod" is her opinion of my lack of walkiness.

So don't feel bad that you weren't striding around the place when you were twelve months old. By all accounts, your old man was just as happy to watch the world go by, or to scoot after it on my belly or ass.

And besides, I'm going to guess that by the time you're reading this (in your teens or twenties or whatever), you've been walking a while and you've no doubt gotten quite good at it. You've probably taken millions of steps by now, some of them better than others, and it doesn't really matter when you took your first one. Knowing where some steps take you in life, there is every chance that the first was never going to be the most important. So, you know what? Not walking yet? Who gives a shit?

~~MILESTONE NO. 6. YOUR FIRST STEPS~~

MILESTONE NO. 6: REALIZING THAT MILESTONES JUST DON'T MATTER AS MUCH AS WE THINK THEY DO

So you're not walking. Big deal.

Around this time, a few weeks before your first birthday, we took you along to a story-and-rhyme morning at our local library, and I listened in on a conversation that two moms were having, each with her own baby in her arms. (I was doing research for this book and not, as your mom suggested, "being a nosy bastard.")

On the surface, this was a polite, friendly conversation about how each of their babies was progressing. But after a while it became clear that the conversation was actually a subtle battleground of one-upmanship.

It went a bit like this:

Mom 1: "So, very excited. Jessica has started to roll over."

Mom 2: "Oh, Elliot was doing that very early. He's actually sitting up on his own now."

Mom 1: "Oh, well, that's good. Jessica's actually showing signs of crawling."

Mom 2: "Well, Elliot is showing signs of standing up. We think he'll be walking early."

Mom 1: "Yes, Jessica seems much more focused on her talking, and everyone says she is very advanced for her age. I notice Elliot's not too chatty."

And so it progressed, with the advancements of each baby exaggerated with every skirmish. I didn't hear the rest of the conversation (we had to leave), but I imagine, at the rate they were exaggerating, I could have returned an hour later to discover that Jessica had become a chess grandmaster, while Elliot had recently delivered a keynote speech to the UN on climate change, before curing diabetes. All of which was made all the more comical by the fact that there these babies lay, in their respective mothers' arms, blissfully clueless, as one quietly shit itself and the other one stared at its own foot as if it were something from space.

So, Charlie, my boy, it is to this conversation that I return, as I think about you not walking. Because it is in this conversation between Jessica's and Elliot's moms that we see the worst in parents: the competitive bullshit that is ever-present, and the way in which "milestones" become the battlegrounds upon which competitive parenting is fought.

As your mom and dad, we tried not to fall for it, but we couldn't help but peer over and measure you against the kids in class who were already crawling, the ones who were already burbling away, or the ones solving Fermat's theorem on a whiteboard in the corner.

As I say, we tried not to fall for it, but all parents do. And, as a consequence of our being drawn into this nonsense, milestones are turned into markers of how our child is progressing, and they become nothing more than inexact measures of how we are performing as a parent. And when a milestone comes along that we don't quite make, we start to worry that we might be doing something wrong. Which is bollocks. Because of course we're doing something wrong . . . but so is everyone else.

The real shame of all this is that milestones become these negative monoliths, mile markers and targets to be hit, rather than what they should be, which is happy flagpoles by the side of the road that we can hang our memories from—memories that, when our little one is old enough, we can share with them . . .

Share with you.

So instead of telling you about your first steps, or any more of the standard tick-a-box moments of your first year, I thought I'd tell you about a couple of milestones that are buried in the grass. Milestones from before you were even born. Milestones that matter. And maybe, when it comes down to it, they are the only ones out of all this lot that really do.

MILESTONE NO. -1 (MINUS ONE): HOW I MET YOUR MOM

I don't doubt that this will come as a crippling shock, but: your dad, as a young man, wasn't a massive hit with the ladies.

I know. Mind. Blown.

I collected comics and enjoyed sci-fi, *Star Wars*, that sort of thing. I even played the role-playing fantasy board game Dungeons and Dragons until well into my teens (I played as a Level 8 Magical Thief by the name of Fagin Swift-hands). And whereas now there is something cool about "geek culture," back then there was no such thing; there were just the "losers." To be a comic-collecting fan of Jedis was to be an outsider, and it was like kryptonite to girls.

The way I looked wasn't bringing a great deal to the party either.

I had my own individual sense of style. My signature look was characterized by center-parted hair down to my shoulders, and a taste for cardigans and band T-shirts. I was also quite skinny and wimpy, and had the fairly unimpressive vital statistics of Kate Moss after a nasty virus. So, with that picture painted, you can see why the possibility of me meeting someone special was quite remote.

But some great romances have remarkable beginnings.

Most don't. And me and your mom's? It didn't. We met in a pub. That's it.

Okay, as anecdotes go, that is pretty shit. But life is not a Richard Curtis film, and I think we should all be pretty glad that it isn't. Because for two people to meet, it doesn't need irony or coincidence or hilarious circumstances. Two people can come together anywhere, at any time, and there is something wonderfully mundane, ordinary, and everyday about it.

So I was standing in The Miner's Arms (that's the name of the pub, I wasn't being cuddled by a miner) in Sheffield. I noticed your mom walk through the door, and I thought she was beautiful.

(. . . I've just taken a minute away from writing the last sentence to use a thesaurus. I wanted to find an alternative word to *beautiful*. A word that seems less sentimental, less overused, less like the name of a Christina Aguilera perfume. But there isn't one. The other options were *pleasing* or *handsome*, which sounds like something you'd say about a cow—"pleasing, handsome, a damn good milker"—I'm just going to leave it at *beautiful*.)

I still remember what your mom was wearing, which I know sounds quite romantic but, I'll be honest, it's not that hard to remember. She was almost all in black. A black jacket, black skirt, black sweater, black tights. But also a pair of aquamarine Adidas Gazelles. In hindsight, she looked like she was attending a funeral but had nipped out for a run. I thought she looked cool as fuck.

But here is where the problem arose. She was cool as fuck, and I wasn't. So when I saw your mom for the first time, it wasn't with a sense of fireworks exploding or music playing in the background, it was with a sinking feeling: that there was no way that she would have any interest in me. No possibility that she would find herself staring back across the pub thinking: *Who is that cool customer with the Jesus hair, shit-brown cardigan, and unmanly body shape of a fourteen-year-old gymnast?*

So when your uncle Oz introduced us, I didn't think: *How can I get this girl to like me?* What I actually thought was: *I really, really hope that this girl is stupid or racist or has a terrible personality or is just an all-round dick. Something that will make me less bothered that I never stood a chance.* It was defeatist, but it was realistic.

But, as we were introduced, she clinked my glass, and we talked for the rest of the night about nothing. Enough nothing that it became clear she was smart and kind. And as she mercilessly ripped the piss out of my cardigan, I thought: *Oh, fuck. She's funny. Damn.*

It was in that moment that I hatched a plan to fool this depressingly dressed girl in the aquamarine Adidas Gazelles into thinking I was way more attractive, smart, interesting, and amusing than I actually was.

I asked her out, she said yes, and against all likelihood the plan worked.

Twenty or so years later, that plan is still going reasonably strong. Although I think she is beginning to suspect that I'm not as smart or funny as I originally made out. (Fortunately, it's too late now; I'm like an old bathrobe that you don't want to part with despite the fact that it's crap.)

When I met your mom, I thought she was a "ten" and that I was a steady "five." But she wasn't the kind of person who cared. (Plus I'm funnier than she is, and everyone gains two points if they can make you laugh. And, as I point out to her sometimes, I'll be able to make her laugh into old age when she looks like a fucking old boot, so the gap's closing.)

Anyway, this was the moment when the two halves of your DNA

collided in a controlled, fairly subdued explosion, and you were placed in fate's mail.

And that's it, as far as you're concerned. Nothing happened, and there wouldn't be another milestone for you for another sixteen years.

When we decided to have a baby.

MILESTONE NO. 0 (ZERO): WE DECIDE TO HAVE A BABY

So, where was I? Right, me and your mom met in a pub. I was drunk enough to ask her out, she was drunk enough to accept, and then nothing happened for sixteen years. Up to speed? Good.

I say nothing happened for sixteen years—that obviously isn't true. I'm just not sure how relevant it is. We traveled a fair bit, bought a house, we got engaged.

We spent those years mostly happy, argued some. Because you argue with the people you love. That's the way it works. (My sister, your aunt Jo, once stabbed me in the leg with a dart over an argument about whether a pop star called Jason Donovan was gay or not. Like I said, you argue with the people you love. A lot.)

Basically, me and your mom spent these sixteen years getting to know each other, and I now know everything about her.

For example, things your mom claims not to be scared of but actually is:

Thunder, lightning, spiders, flying, needles, daddy longlegs, the voices that people make when they inhale helium, leaving her supermarket cart unattended (even though she hasn't paid for the contents yet, she still thinks someone will steal it), and bats.

She also claims not to be superstitious, but won't cross on the stairs and won't put shoes on the table—and if she sees a magpie, she salutes it and whispers under her breath: "Good morning, Mister Magpie" (I'm not even sure that's a thing).

And because she is so much more together, and less flaky, than me, the things that I came to love about her more than anything are her imperfections. I love the fact that she pronounces the word *avocado* with an extra *d*, like "advocado." And I love the fact that when she reads this bit, she'll go apeshit that I told everyone that she pronounces the word *avocado* wrong.

Basically, before you came along, we were happy and had a pretty good life. We didn't really talk about having kids. Weirdly, it just didn't come up that often, and as we got older I think we both just kind of assumed that we wouldn't have any.

Then one morning in 2009, I got a phone call from my dad, your granddad Gerald. He sounded kind of confused, and he stumblingly explained that he wasn't feeling too well. That morning, he'd been in church, and when asked to do a reading he found himself halfway through and unable to concentrate. The words were spidering across the page and he couldn't quite focus. Worried, we took him off to the hospital, and after a few days of tests, it turned out that he was more unwell than we thought and he had a type of cancer that had spread to his brain.

(Note: if you're not Charlie and you're reading this, I know what you're thinking: Wow, this lighthearted book on parenting just took a serious left turn. Thanks a lot, Matt—two pages ago I was having fun, and now I feel like putting my head in the fucking oven. *Well, don't turn on the gas just yet. Because this is the story of how Charlie came to be.)*

There are times for all of us when circumstance will plunge its fist into your chest, tear out your heart, and show it to you, pink and beating. And for the year that my dad had left, as a family we were hollowed out. I miss your granddad a lot, and it feels like something is out of kilter with reality that you and he will never meet. You'd have gotten along.

But in the months he had left, we talked a lot about us as father and son. He apologized a lot for the mistakes he'd made as a parent. There weren't any, but he apologized anyway. I apologized for my mistakes as a son. There were plenty, but he pretended there weren't. And he talked about how he had come to terms with what was to come because his kids were settled and happy.

These were strange conversations. Maybe it's because when you're talking to someone who is dying, everything they say seems somehow profound and worth listening to.

What these conversations did, though, was make me see parenthood slightly differently. Your granddad was still a young man at the time of his diagnosis, and so had been given a pretty shitty deal. But he accepted that deal more easily because his children were happy, and I thought that a curious thing. There was no way, placed in his position, I could have so easily accepted such a raw fate, just because another human (even one that I was related to) was okay.

I started to realize that being a parent was defined by an odd sort of selflessness, an unselfishness I just didn't have, and that the relationship between a parent and his or her kid was a genuinely unique one. And that maybe, as I lost one relationship to the great nothing, the closest I would ever come to finding it again would be from the other side of that equation as a dad to a son or daughter.

So when your granddad died, this experience, these conversations, and this new wisdom got scooped up with the feelings of mortality that come along with a parent dying. Your mom was close to your granddad, and she felt the same way, and all of this stuff was smashed together to make us realize that it might be quite good if you were in our lives.

In the weeks after your granddad died, me and your mom had that conversation: the one that cemented our decision to try for a baby. And in that moment, we felt like we had called out to the universe, and you, our Charlie, boarded a big, fuck-off white egg, like Superman leaving his home planet, and you would crash-land into our lives at your earliest convenience.

It didn't work that way. The universe was an uncooperative shit-head.

It would be four years before you landed. Four years of disappointments and defeats, false starts and sometimes brutal sadness. And your absence began to feel like a weight belt. But your mom is determined, and I'm Disney-optimistic, and we didn't give up.

Like so many parents for whom having kids is not straightforward, every time we walked into the wood-chipper of disappointment, we walked out the other side, bloodied but determined to reassemble ourselves and keep going. With no guarantees, nothing like simple certainty.

Then you happened. Your Superman egg appeared on the radar. Faint at first, but a clear blip. We wouldn't get carried away or get our hopes up, but it was there, blipping away, and as you got closer, the blipping got stronger.

And three months after you announced that you were on your way (in the beautifully inauspicious guise of a smiley emoticon on a piss-covered plastic stick) . . . we saw you on a screen, and the moment that we saw your black-and-white feet and a grainy middle finger, it felt like something perfect.

And it was.

Dad xxx

10

JUDGMENTS
AND REVELATIONS

A Parent's Prayer:
  *May we give you hope, curiosity, compassion, and love . . . but
fuck things up, just enough to make you interesting.*

JUDGMENTS
AND REVELATIONS

When I think about the last year and what it's like to become a parent for the first time, I'm reminded of standing in my back garden one night a few years ago. It was the night of a Perseid meteor shower: a particularly clear evening that saw shooting stars, one after another, blaze across the sky in a breathtaking, majestic, and humbling cosmic display. It was a night that made you think about your place in the universe and consider the big philosophical questions about humanity and life and everything.

And in my line of sight that evening was next door's cat, sitting on our back fence, noisily licking its own ass.

That's the closest thing I can think of to the contrasting experiences of being a parent to a newborn baby: always in your line of sight is the mundane, sometimes disgusting, day-to-day grind of crap and snot and vomit and sleeplessness. But, as unpleasant as all this stuff can be, it just doesn't diminish the fact that, all the while, something incredible is happening, something that makes you reconsider your place in the universe and everything else.

So, whether you're standing in your back garden distracted by an ass-licking cat or you're standing in a nursery staring at a sleepless night and an overflowing diaper bin, all the while this magical, extraordinary thing goes on. The trick is to remember to look up every now and again.

But that can be easier said than done.

REVELATIONS I:
BEING A NEW PARENT IS HARD

I am not great parent material.

I am, and always have been, lazy. I take very few things seriously. I am disorganized and lacking in anything approaching common sense. I am immature: just last night I made a salad for dinner and on the plate arranged Lyndsay's two tomatoes and mini-cucumber so that they looked like a cock and balls:

I am forgetful, frequently dim, and something of an inept and clueless fuckup. And so, for these reasons and a thousand others, becoming a parent hit me like a hammer made of hammers.

In my defense, I think the reality of being a parent for the first time comes as a shock to most people. Everybody tells you it's going to be hard, so it really shouldn't come as any great surprise when it is. But that jolt comes anyway: because it *is* hard.

JUDGMENTS AND REVELATIONS

A friend of ours sent us a note when Charlie was born. It said that our lives were about to change forever, and to prepare for a "gear change." And becoming a parent for the first time *is* a gear change— a seriously grinding, metal-on-metal, shrieking gear change. And in the beginning it feels less like changing gears and more like the car you are in has plunged off a cliff, rolled several times, and then burst into flames before coming to a stop halfway up a tree.

For those first few months you are just as much an infant as the one you brought home from the hospital. You have to learn a new language and new skills, and adjust to a new world that bears no resemblance to the old one.

And no allowances are made for the fact that you are also a baby, disoriented and confused. No allowance is made for how unready you might be. There is no slow-learners class (like that class at school for those kids who weren't ready for scissors); you just have to keep up, and keeping up can be tough.

But human beings, even ones as pathetically ill-equipped as I am, are resourceful and smart. Our capacity for change is an evolutionary birthday cake. And once you learn some of the basics, adjust to your new reality, and ascertain that you can't actually die from a lack of sleep (I mean, you can, but you probably won't), you do what humans have done for millennia: you adapt. Maybe you even begin to get the hang of it.

Make no mistake, after those initial months, it still remains hard, exhausting, confusing, and all those things. But slowly, as the weeks and months pass, you realize something: the moments that are terrible are getting shorter and the moments of joy are getting longer.

Until, one day, you start to feel like a parent, and less like you want to drink lighter fluid, run into the wilderness, and never ever look back.

REVELATIONS II:
ALMOST ALL NEW-PARENT ADVICE IS SHIT

So becoming a parent is hard. What should make it easier, though, is that billions of people before you have already done it. There is no shortage of experience upon which to draw. No limit to the amount of useful advice out there to make your path easier and more straight-forward. Or at least, that's what I thought before we had Charlie.

In reality, after a year as a dad, I have reached the same conclusion that most other parents reach: the vast majority of parenting advice is shit and, for all intents and purposes, about as useful as this drawing of a dinosaur enjoying a yo-yo:

The problem is that advice for new parents is a mixture of old wives' tales, scientific trends, subjective experience, and plain old bollocks, all wrapped up as knowledge, wisdom, and fact. When, in truth, most of the time it's just opinion. And everyone has an opinion, and usually more than one.

It's a tired old saying, but it is true: opinions are like assholes because everyone's got one. But when it comes to parenting, everyone seems to have seven assholes, and they are constantly thrusting them in your face, whether you're interested in their assholes or not.

Some of these opinions are well intentioned, and some of them are cruel and stupid. Some are wrapped in expensive-looking book covers, and some are shared over a cup of tea. But one thing that there isn't, is a shortage. And that's an issue. There is just so much advice and opinion that it is overwhelming, and sorting through it all is impossible.

Way back in Chapter 1, I mentioned that there were more than thirty thousand books on pregnancy and childbirth on the market. But there are more than a hundred thousand different how-to parenting books telling you what to do once the baby is here. And, scrolling through them all on Amazon, I think it's a shame that the Nazis, Stalin, and McCarthyism have given book-burning such a bad name, because a case can be made for making a big bonfire of most of them. (And a fine fire it would be: a hundred thousand books would be a few miles high, and a fire that big could be seen from space, probably by aliens wondering why they could smell the distinct aroma of burning bullshit.)

I'm not really suggesting a book-burning (unless you've got a copy of the loathsome Katie Hopkins's 2013 opus *The Class Book of Baby Names,* in which case, have at it). And there are no doubt some great, useful books out there, ones that don't pretend to have all the answers.

But even if you had time to read every single one of the hundred thousand books available, see every documentary ever made, and study every scientific paper ever published, the chances are that you would finish more confused than when you started. Because as well as the sheer volume of opinion, you also have to deal with the fact that the advice is confusing as fuck and, from the experts to the nanas, everyone seems to disagree with one another.

Take something as simple as whether or not to allow your baby to have a pacifier. The advice about this simple decision ranges from:

A pacifier is vital for sleeping safety and soothing a tired baby.

to:

A pacifier will give you a cross-eyed, bucktoothed baby who won't form a word until they are in their late thirties.

(Neither is true: pacifiers aren't "vital" because a lot of babies don't have them. And they won't turn your baby into a toothy fuckwit either, because most babies actually do have them and they turn out fine.)

So where is the useful information and advice that can be fished out of the toilet of that particular debate?

This is just one example. As we've already seen, it is also true of advice about sleep training, breast-feeding, TV, weaning, and anything else that you can think of. All of these issues are the subject of contradictory arguments and disagreement. And the only conclusion a new parent can reach is this: actually, no one knows much of anything for sure.

The thing is, I can't help thinking that there is a pretty obvious reason why no one knows much of anything for sure. Why there is so much contradiction and disagreement and no agreed-upon, right-or-wrong way of doing things.

Maybe it's just because one size does not fit all.

Babies aren't cause-and-effect machines; they are complicated. Each one is unique, maddeningly so. Because they are human beings, and humans are annoyingly individual.

It's why some people like to be hung upside down from their nipples and other people like a nice sandwich and an afternoon playing bingo. We are all different, and that seems to be true from birth, from the moment we take our first breath. So the idea that there is such a thing as a step-by-step guide to raising a baby, a right or a wrong way to do it, or that what worked for Aunt Eileen is guaranteed to work for you, is just wrong.

REVELATIONS III:
PARENTAL INSTINCTS ARE A REAL THING

So wading through the torrent of advice available, and trying to sort the good advice from the bad, is pretty much impossible. The only alternative is to just trust your own instincts.

JUDGMENTS AND REVELATIONS

As the venerable Dr. Spock says at the very start of his book *Baby and Child Care*:

Trust yourself, you know more than you think.

(Of course, he ruined all that by writing another 540 pages about why you should trust him instead, but still, the sentiment is there.)

I always assumed that the idea of "parental instincts" was nonsense. Just pseudo-scientific crap. Whenever people say "trust your instincts" about anything else, it tends to be complete bollocks. I once had a boss who had a sign above his desk that said that success at work was 99 percent trusting your instincts. And that never sounded right to me, especially given that every morning when *I* get up to go to work, my instincts are to fuck it off and sit around all day in my underwear eating Pringles.

"Trust your gut" is a nice, neat idea, but I've never thought that it was anything more than the sort of fortune-cookie philosophy that includes "go with your heart" or "release yourself from your past."

So it was a genuine revelation for me to discover that parental instincts are a real thing: instincts that seem to lie dormant until called upon by parenthood. And when you learn to trust them, they make the opinions of others seem like white dogshit: pale, chalky, and seldom useful.

When people talk about parental instincts, what they are usually talking about are maternal instincts. And maternal instincts really are something to behold: they are alive and tough and they don't take any shit. Lyndsay's maternal instincts were there before our baby was even showing as a bump, and expressed themselves with the instinct to nest and buy all that stuff we didn't need. And her instincts to nurture and provide, and sacrifice everything for Charlie, were all alive and well on the day that he was born.

One year on, those maternal instincts continue to grow, with the ability to instinctively recognize what Charlie needs or why he is upset. Which is a mom-ability that I have always found impressive, given that those reasons can range from teething and tiredness to the fact that there are too many bubbles in his bath or you would like him to wear a hat.

I'll be honest: as a dad, it's not an ability I've mastered. Consequently, me and Lyns have slightly different methods for assessing why Charlie might be unhappy:

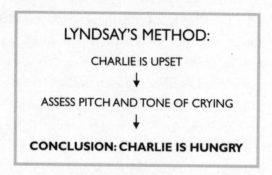

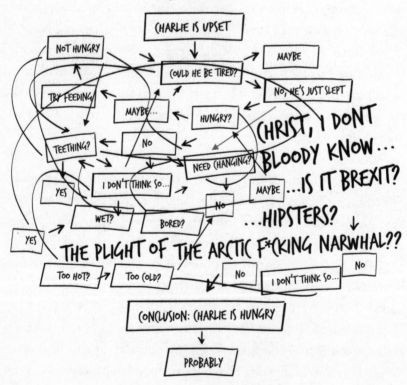

For me, maternal instincts are a strange wizardry. But paternal instincts do exist as well. It's fair to say that I have the same instincts for recognizing what is upsetting Charlie, but the truth is that the volume on that intuition is turned down a bit, and I accept that it is just not as accurate as Lyndsay's more telepathic approach.

That said, I definitely feel the same powerful instincts to nurture, sacrifice for, and provide for Charlie.

I have even developed a protective streak.

Just last week, I punched a seagull. In the face.

It's not something I'm proud of. We were having a day at the beach, and as Charlie was enjoying his ice cream, he was dive-bombed by an aggressive seagull, and I instinctively reacted and punched it. In the face.

In my forty-odd years on this planet, I have never been in a fight or kicked a dog. I scoop up spiders in a plastic tub and, when I take them out to the garden, I find a comfortable spot to release them. Yet now I find myself the sort of person who decks seabirds because they show an interest in my son's ice cream.

And the worst thing is . . . I'd do it again. In fact, Mr. Seagull, tell your pals, bring a whole flock. Come near my son's Cornetto and I will take on all you fucking beaky bastards!?

Like I said . . . I've developed a protective streak.

. . .

So an accidentally recurring theme in this book has been the baffling nature of expert advice and opinion. But, weirdly, I've just stumbled across another quote from Dr. Spock in *Baby and Child Care* that reveals something of the truth:

> *It may surprise you to hear that the more people have studied different methods of bringing up children, the more they have come to the conclusion that what good mothers and fathers instinctively feel like doing for their babies is usually best.*

Maybe we'll save Spock from the fire after all.

Certainly if I've learned anything at all in the last year, it's something close to this. There are no shortcuts, no simple answers, and very few tricks to adjusting to parenthood . . . apart from one. A shortcut, answer, and trick that I wish had been impressed upon us from the very start. A simple advisory note that should be a motto for all those carrying their newborn nervously from the labor ward to their car, and a caveat at the front of every book on babies ever written:

Trust your instincts, because they are worthy of your trust.

Even if that means decking a bird.

REVELATIONS IV:
THE PERFECT PARENT IS A MYTH

For most people, I think it's the point at which you start ignoring advice and opinions and start trusting your instincts that you begin to feel like you are getting the hang of this parenting stuff.

But that doesn't mean you suddenly have all the answers. Christ, it doesn't even mean you necessarily understand the questions. You don't overnight become the "perfect parent." No one does. Because, despite what you may have heard, there's no such thing.

Try to conjure an image of the perfect parent in your mind. (This person will most likely be a woman. Expectations of men are way, way lower.) Perhaps it's a celebrity or a real person, a friend even, whom you see sharing their perfection on Facebook or Instagram. That person, no doubt, seems to glide through parenthood without a hair out of place. They spend their mornings weaving their children's clothes out of hemp and dandelions, their afternoons making rice pudding out of breast milk. They are never unkempt, never tired, never frustrated, and always fucking baking.

And they are con artists. Look closer. Look into their eyes and you will see the lie. These are the calm swans whose feet are frantically pedaling beneath the surface. For every staged photo of contained messy play and baked organic muffins fresh out of the oven, just out of shot you can be sure that there is a baby screaming the world in two and a toddler forcing a mashed-up cookie into a dog's ass.

How many of these parentally perfect creatures have you actually seen, up close and in real life, in their actual habitat? I'm not talking about on social media. I'm talking about at four o'clock in the morning, when their baby has chicken pox and is projectile-vomiting up the Orla Kiely stem-print curtains.

The perfect parent isn't real. It's a fiction that just does not bear scrutiny. It's like the Loch Ness monster: even if you think you see one from a distance, you get up close, and it's just a pair of old tires and a shopping cart.

The problem with this fake ideal is that it is far from harmless. In fact, it's poison. There is an entire industry of lifestyle philosophies and celebrity-fueled culture built around this myth. And it really is the worst kind of myth. The perfect parent is an insidious, fictional bogeyman, an imaginary monster designed to scare parents into thinking they're fucking everything up. That they're not good enough. That they are inadequate. That there is an ideal out there somewhere that they just do not measure up to.

I don't feel like this. I mean, I feel inadequate, but I don't feel bad about it. The baseline of expectation for dads really is so much lower than it is for moms. There is considerably less pressure to be an über-parent when you happen to have a penis. No one expects men to bake, in kitten heels, while teaching a baby "phonics." Men get credit for just generally being around and quietly high-five themselves for being the kind of guy who changes a diaper. (Yes, it's 2018; yes, it's ridiculous; yes, it's true.)

But Lyns, and every other mom I have ever spoken to, has felt this specter of inadequacy at some point, and felt it keenly. A sense that they are failing their little one, or that they should be finding the whole thing . . . easier. And it's nonsense. A nonsense that can all be traced back to this high ideal of the perfect parent. A bullshit fantasy.

I have no idea what the answer is—how not to fall for this particular lie. I suppose the only thing parents can do is to try not to measure themselves against anything other than the happiness of their own family. If it's a celebrity mom you imagine when you conjure the image of the perfect parent, imagine too the area outside the flimsy set and the entourage of nannies and makeup artists required to make a celebrity mom look as if parenting is a breeze.

And those noncelebrity "friends" and acquaintances who perpetuate the myth with the smoke and mirrors of their own closely cropped photos? Try not to judge them too harshly. As annoying as they may be, they deserve your pity. Maintaining an illusion like this is tough, and they are lost in the myth themselves.

LOCH NESS MONSTER   BIGFOOT   JABBERWOCKY   UNICORN   PERFECT PARENT

REVELATIONS V:
IN FACT, EVERYONE IS A SHIT PARENT

Maybe I'm wrong and there is such a thing as the Perfect Parent. But, if there is, no one can agree on what the fuck one looks like. So who cares? In fact, no one can quite agree on what it is to be a good parent, let alone a perfect one. You may be reading this thinking: *Well, I know I am a good parent.* And maybe you are and maybe you're not. I'm not really in a position to comment. But one thing that I am absolutely certain of is that you are a bad parent. In fact, you are a terrible parent.

. . . According to somebody.

In 2015, fashion chimps Dolce and Gabbana gave a magazine interview in which fashion chimp number one, Dolce, commented about the wrongness of same-sex parenting. He said that "the only family is the traditional one," and that IVF children were just "children of chemistry" and "synthetic."

Don't get me wrong: Who gives a fuck what Dolce or Gabbana thinks about anything? They make clothes. And listening to their opinions on IVF is like paying close attention to what Topshop thinks about stem-cell research.

But there is something striking about these comments: they are opinions about whether someone is fit to be a parent before their little one is even born—a declaration that a parent (or a child) can be good or bad before a sperm has even met an egg. And isn't that an incredible thing? That you can be judged a bad parent when your baby is nothing more than an idea?

The point being, if it's possible to be judged as a parent when your baby is just a thought, it is little wonder that once parents have their baby in their arms, they can find themselves under siege from opinions suggesting that they themselves are "bad parents."

The Dolce and Gabbana example is an extreme one, but it's not just gay parents or the parents of IVF babies who face these judgments. We all do. You could be as straight as it's possible to be, your little one "naturally conceived" outside a lab and against the back wall of a shed. It doesn't matter; there is no escape. There is always a reason why you are unfit to be a parent.

I myself have had a number of people pointing out the reasons why I am unfit. I'm sure you are gripping this book a little harder in shock, but, yes, even me. (Actually, when you blog about this sort of stuff, it tends to invite this kind of opinion. I can't say I mind. I've come to collect these odd messages like badges: little reminders that the world is full of lovably acidic piss-monkeys.)

So, for the record, here are one or two examples of messages I've received letting me know why *I* am a bad parent. (Along with my responses.)

I am too sweary:

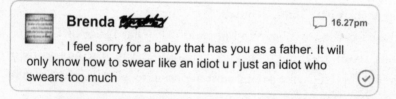

Brenda ~~Huxbby~~   🗨 16.27pm

I feel sorry for a baby that has you as a father. It will only know how to swear like an idiot u r just an idiot who swears too much   ✓

Matt Coyne   🗨 18.42pm

Aww, Thanks Brenda. It's true the swearing is a problem... We were unsure as to whether Charlie's first words would be 'mummy' or 'daddy' but we have now decided to teach him so that his first words are "piss up a rope Brenda, you dismal fucktrumpet".

All the best, Matt x   ✓

I am too stupid:

Michael ~~Newby~~   11.21pm

You are one dumb asshole, How did you ever become a parent? Who the hell agreed to have sex with you??? even once??

Matt Coyne   11.32pm

Your Gran?

Michael ~~Newby~~   11.35pm

wow hilarious - really mature

Matt Coyne   11.42pm

Yes she is... But, in fairness she goes like a dog at a gate.

I am contributing to climate change?

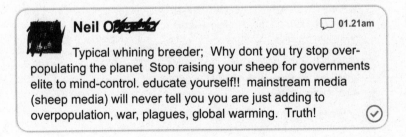

Neil O~~Reilly~~   01.21am

Typical whining breeder; Why dont you try stop over-populating the planet Stop raising your sheep for governments elite to mind-control. educate yourself!! mainstream media (sheep media) will never tell you you are just adding to overpopulation, war, plagues, global warming. Truth!

Yeah, I'm not daft. I didn't reply to that one. But I did send him this picture of me wearing a tinfoil hat:

Matt Coyne   💬 11.22am

And, finally, I am too old:

Greg ~~Horsley~~   💬 12.31pm

No wonder you cant cope what an idiot is ridiculuos to have a baby when you are 41 old, 35 is even to old Its is cruel and quiet selfsh. I had my chidren when I was twentys and yes now im in 30s this means I can myselftake care of them!! and not relay on everyone else because Im then to old.

Matt Coyne   💬 18.39pm

Hi Greg, thanks for getting in touch! Apologies for taking a while to respond to your comment. I was trying to decipher the language used? Apparently, it is English... although to be honest if you're going to write an insulting rant it would probably be more effective if the receiver didn't need one of those enigma code-breaking machines to work out what the fuck you're talking about. (Seriously, did you type this with your hands or just bash your sloping forehead against the keyboard until what you thought looked like a sentence appeared on screen?)

Anyway, just wanted to let you know I've taken your well-thought-out and reasoned opinion on board and come to the conclusion that, even though you had your children in your twenties, I suspect that your kids would prefer a father of any age rather than an opinionated halfwit with the IQ of yeast... and such a large stick up his ass he is, to all intents and purposes... a tree.

All the best, Matt x

These are just a few examples. But of all the many reasons I have heard for why I'm a bad parent, the age one is the most interesting, and it's also the one I hear most often. Just to clarify: as I write this, I'm forty-two, not the same age as Yoda. I'm not sitting at home watching *Murder, She Wrote* with a blanket on my legs, banging on about the war. But for a sizable number of commentators, forty seems to be some sort of cutoff point, beyond which apparently you're just too close to death to be a parent.

I even had a woman commenting that forty was definitely too old to be a parent because, "as a teacher," she'd seen the heartbreak caused "when an older parent dies, leaving the school-age child devastated." Well, I hope this woman doesn't teach fucking math. Because, by my reckoning, if I live to the average age of eighty-five, Charlie will be forty-odd by the time I cark it. So if he's still in school and in short trousers then, he's got bigger problems.

The truth is that, as a parent, there is no escape from petty judgments. For these people, I am too old to be a good dad—and while you may be in the flush of youth, for some of these broken, bitter few, you will no doubt be too young or too poor, too easygoing or too cautious, too married, too unmarried, too gay, too mumsy or too unmumsy, too disorganized or too obsessive, maybe you work or maybe you don't work, etc., etc. No one is immune. Make no mistake: someone somewhere thinks you are a bad parent.

Not to worry.

The logic of most of these opinions is enough to make your brain cry. And if you come across someone who measures a parent not by their care and love, but by their age, gender, bank balance, or sexuality, by whether their child is IVF, or whatever, then you're most likely dealing with a dribbling idiot, a person capable of all the considered thoughtfulness of a potato.

These attitudes seem like simplistic views of parenthood, but the really idiotic thing? The truth is actually so much *more* simple, and every shred of evidence proves it: all of this stuff is irrelevant. If you love and care about your kid, the chances are that they will become the best of you. If you don't, they won't.

That's it.

So link arms with the bad parent to your left, take the hand of the shitty parent to your right, and with one voice tell the "someone somewheres" that they are welcome to go fuck themselves. And as for Greg, you, sir, can kiss my aging balls.

REVELATIONS VI:
THE MYSTERY AND THE MADNESS

Twelve months ago, the night before Charlie was born, I had a dream: I dreamed that I was a soldier riding into battle, completely naked, and on the back of a large, inflatable duck. I think my subconscious was basically taking the piss about how unprepared I was for the new arrival.

It turns out my subconscious was absolutely right and the inflatable-duck dream quite prophetic. I really wasn't prepared. For any of it.

And so when I hear other parents talk about how their first year of parenthood just flew by, I wonder if they are lying or are suffering from some sort of post-traumatic stress and have blanked out what actually happened.

For me, the last year hasn't flown by at all. It's been the longest year of my life.

A year ago I had a few wrinkles, a few gray hairs, and now I'm aging so fast that by the time Charlie's ten years old I'm going to look a lot like Gandalf's balls. I have the back of a 120-year-old Japanese woman. My hair is thinning, and I have bags under my eyes that look like a bloodhound's weekly shopping. And if I remember to shave and shower in the same day, I consider that a day of singular triumph.

Aside from my physical wreckage, I am also mentally coming

apart at the seams. I am so sleep-deprived that I *still* occasionally hallucinate that my long-dead great-grandma Rose is taking a shit in our downstairs bathroom. And this lack of sleep, coupled with poor diet and the ongoing nightmare of kids' TV, means that my mind is basically Play-Doh. And, on a day-to-day basis, without caffeine I am incapable of anything more complicated than blinking or scratching my arse.

So after an entire year as a parent, I find myself changed. But the main way in which I'm changed is that I'm happier. It sounds dopey, after all this, to put it so simply. But when Charlie made his entrance, and we eyed each other suspiciously that very first time, I wasn't expecting to be quite so taken with our little human. I didn't realize that I would become so superglue-attached, or quite so enthusiastic and proud when he laughs or waves or does something else that, objectively, isn't that earth-shatteringly impressive but feels like it is.

The past twelve months have been baffling, humbling, exhausting, terrible, and ideal. I'd love to say that I've learned a great deal, but that would be a lie. I still don't know whether swaddling is a good or a bad thing, how to keep Charlie's socks on for more than a nanosecond, or how to stop a baby, mid-change, from dipping a hand in his own crap like it's tapas.

But that's okay.

Apparently, Thomas Moore once said: "It is only through mystery and madness that the soul is revealed," and maybe that's true.

The one thing of importance that I have learned in the past year is actually something just as profound:

When it comes to Charlie and his mom, I would ride into battle, naked, and on the back of a large inflatable duck . . . without hesitation.

ACKNOWLEDGMENTS

Does anyone ever read this bit? I'm not sure anyone ever reads this bit. I never read this bit. In future I think I will though, because it's only now that I come to write this bit that I realize how important it is. This book wouldn't exist without the help and support of a bunch of people . . . and if it did exist, it would be about seven pages long and consist mainly of doodles of me bashing my head against the floor.

I need to thank my agent at A. M. Heath, Euan Thorneycroft—who has the surname of a heartless, Dickensian slum landlord but is actually a thoroughly decent fella. I can't thank him enough for guiding me through the publishing process with good humor and beer and for taking on my sorry ass in the first place. Thank you to the family Wildfire: my UK editor Alex Clarke, Kate Stephenson, and part human/part firework Ella Gordon. Thank you all so much for helping to turn the musings of an idiot into something that looks an awful lot like a book. And thanks too to all at Headline: Caitlin Raynor, Jo Liddiard, and Frances Gough. A truly formidable marketing team fueled in part by Moscow Mules and Herman ze German takeaway sausage.

A very special thank-you to all at Scribner —Nan Graham, Colin Harrison, Roz Lippel, Brian Belfiglio, Jaya Miceli, Ryan Raphael, Jill Putorti, Dan Cuddy, Hailey Rutledge, and Sally Howe—and in particular to my mighty US editor and champion, the incomparable Valerie Steiker. It is often said that the US and the UK have a "special relationship," but if it ever breaks down the American government should appoint Valerie to be its ambassador to Britain. Her enthusiasm, patience, and good humor during the whole process of bringing *Man vs. Baby* from the UK to the US has made the ocean between us seem like a pesky puddle. I can only apologize for teaching her profanities that no woman of her charm and distinction should know.

A huge thank-you to my friends and family. In particular, Lyndsay's mom and dad, who dropped everything countless times to help out with Charlie when I was on deadline. Ron, Lorraine, I cannot express my gratitude strongly enough for everything you do. And thank you too to my little sis, Jo, and her man, Paul, for their own babysitting duties, and their persistent enthusiasm and encouragement. Of course, thank you to my mum, who not only taught me the value of books but is responsible for selling more copies of this one than anyone . . . banging on about it to anyone who would listen. She is a proud mum but also a pragmatist. In her own words: "Look, Matthew, if you have a successful writing career, maybe I can look forward to a room in a nursing home with a window and not one that smells of urine and cabbage." She dreams big, my ma.

When it comes to acknowledging Lyns's and Charlie's role in all this, "thank you" is an inadequate expression of the gratitude I feel for this last year. Lyndsay, Charlie: the good bits in this book, the bits that are heartfelt and the best of me . . . those bits are yours. I will indeed love you until my spine is dust.

Finally I want to say a massive, genuine thank-you to all of you who follow and comment and contribute to *Man vs. Baby*. It's largely down to you lot that I was given this opportunity in the first place, and I will be forever in your debt. . . . I promise, if we ever meet in person, I will buy each and every one of you a drink.* I have had the privilege over this past year of sharing not just my own experience of becoming a parent but also sharing in yours. And through that experience, I've come to realize that there are many, many parents out there who are trying to raise their kids to be smart and funny and

---

*(Not in any way legally binding.)

ACKNOWLEDGMENTS

fair, tolerant and good . . . and to not be total fucking dicks to one another. Because of that, you make me feel overwhelmingly positive about dispatching my own tiny human into a sometimes uncertain future. And I thank you for that more than anything.

Matt Coyne, Sheffield, UK

(I've put the location because I always think it makes it sound like the author is slowly and with satisfaction laying down a quill and staring wistfully into the distance. In reality, as I write this last word I'm sitting in the Sheffield city center branch of Starbucks, eating a cream horn and wondering whether to tell a chap standing outside the window that a bird's just shit in his hood.)

ABOUT THE AUTHOR

MATT COYNE is a fortysomething-year-old graphic designer from Sheffield, England. In September 2015, Matt's life was turned upside-down by the arrival of his first child, Charlie. After three months of fatherhood, he logged on to Facebook and wrote about his experience of suddenly having to live with "a furious, sleep-murdering, unstable and incontinent, breasts-obsessed midget lodger." Within days, his post about surviving the first few months of parenthood became a viral sensation and was shared all over the world. He continues to impart his parental triumphs and disasters on his blog, *Man vs. Baby*.

Facebook: /manversusbaby
Instagram: manversusbaby
Twitter: @mattcoyney
www.man-vs-baby.co.uk